Grammar and Usage
Workbook

Grade 10

McDougal Littell
A HOUGHTON MIFFLIN COMPANY
Evanston, Illinois • Boston • Dallas

Special Features of the Grammar and Usage Workbook

- It contains a wealth of skill-building exercises in grammar, usage, capitalization, and punctuation.

- Each page focuses on one topic or skill. A brief instructional summary is followed by comprehensive reinforcement exercises.

- Key words and phrases are highlighted for greater clarity and ease of use.

- Each page corresponds to a part in the pupil text for easy reference.

- Grammar lessons are leveled. Form A introduces the skill. Form B extends the skill with more advanced exercises.

- Skills Assessment sheets may be used by the student for self-diagnosis and additional practice or by the teacher as a check for understanding.

- A proofreading practice activity is provided for each Grammar and Usage Handbook.

Printed in the United States of America.

ISBN-13: 978-0-395-86395-4   ISBN-10: 0-395-86395-3

8 9 10 11 12 –MDO– 11 10 09 08 07

Contents

Grammar and Usage Handbook

Nouns

A **noun** is a word that names a person, place, thing, or idea. There are several types of nouns.

Common Noun	a general name for a person, place, thing, or idea
Proper Noun	the name of a particular person, place, thing, or idea; proper nouns are always capitalized.
Concrete Noun	a noun that can be perceived through the senses (*paper, bread, radio*)
Abstract Noun	a noun that cannot be perceived through the senses (*loyalty, happiness, frustration*)
Compound Noun	a noun that contains two or more shorter words; written as one word, separate words, or with hyphens (*grandfather, compact disc, son-in-law*)
Collective Noun	a singular noun referring to a group of people or things (*class, flock*)

A. Identifying Nouns

Underline the nouns in the following sentences.

1. Benjamin Franklin invented bifocals.

2. A molecule of water has two atoms of hydrogen and one atom of oxygen.

3. Fireworks were set off after he hit the winning home run.

4. Parents and children need to develop relationships based on trust.

5. The audience cheered wildly at the end of the concert.

B. Identifying Common, Proper, Concrete, and Abstract Nouns

Identify the boldfaced nouns as common or proper. Write **C** or **P** above the noun. Then write **concrete** or **abstract** in the blank.

1. An anthropologist wrote about the *beliefs* of the Samoans. _____

2. Pablo Picasso was a great *artist.* _____

3. In ancient *Rome,* contests were held in the Colosseum. _____

4. Superman espoused "truth, *justice,* and the American way." _____

5. The story of Odysseus' journey is a product of Homer's vivid *imagination.* _____

6. *Peter the Great* made Russia into a powerful nation. _____

7. The *planet* Mercury is closer than Mars to the sun. _____

8. The British statesman Neville Chamberlain promised "*peace* in our time" just before the outbreak of World War II. _____

9. Before the arrival of *Europeans,* the people of North and South America had developed hundreds of rich cultures. _____

10. Emily Dickinson's poetry is notable for its *clarity* and precision. _____

Nouns

A. Identifying Nouns

Label each boldfaced noun as common (**C**), proper (**P**), abstract (**A**), concrete (**CT**), compound (**CD**), and/or collective (**CL**) by writing the appropriate letters above it. Use two labels for each noun.

1. The **nation** of Australia, like the American nation, was founded by **people** who had rejected, or been rejected by, **Europeans**.

2. For **thousands** of years before the European settlers arrived, a **group** of native people, the **Aborigines**, had the vast **area** of Australia to itself.

3. The **settlers** of Australia treated the Aborigines as unjustly as the settlers of North and South America treated the **Native Americans.**

4. The **Australians**, like the American **colonists**, experimented with the **ideas** of **egalitarianism** and **democracy**.

5. The government the Australians founded has a **prime minister** and **lawmakers** who meet in a **legislature** called the Federal Parliament.

6. Although it is about the same **size** as the continental **United States**, Australia's population density averages only five people per **square mile.**

B. Using Nouns

Replace each boldfaced noun in the list with the type of noun specified in parentheses. The new noun should reflect the same idea or subject as the boldfaced noun.

> Examples   **vegetable** (compound)   **green bean**
>   **snow** (abstract)   **meteorology**

1. **Christopher Columbus** (common) _____

2. **holiday** (proper) _____

3. **players** (collective) _____

4. **building** (compound) _____

5. **state** (proper) _____

6. **North America** (abstract) _____

7. **recreation** (concrete) _____

8. **cattle** (collective) _____

9. **worker** (compound) _____

Pronouns (I)

A **pronoun** is a word used in place of a noun or another pronoun. Three types of pronouns are described below.

Personal pronouns	change form to express person, number, gender, and possession (*I, me, my, mine; you, your, yours; he, him, his; she, her, hers; it, its; we, us, our, ours; they, them, their, theirs*)
Demonstrative pronouns	point out persons or things (*this, that, these those*)
Reflexive and Intensive pronouns	end in *-self* or *-selves;* **reflexive pronouns** reflect action back to the subject; **intensive** pronouns add emphasis (*myself, yourself, himself, herself, itself, ourselves, yourselves, themselves*)

A. Identifying Pronouns

Underline the personal and demonstrative pronouns in the following sentences.

1. This is a movie about astronauts lost in space.

2. Did you leave my history notes on the desk?

3. These are the new fees for long-distance calls.

4. Mr. Black told Kathy he would give her a job in his store.

5. The club members approved the treasurer's report as soon as they heard it.

6. Although Elaine is only six years old, she can already use a computer.

7. The satisfied diner exclaimed, "That tasted great!"

8. The electrician brought all of his equipment into our house.

B. Using Reflexive and Intensive Pronouns

Write an acceptable reflexive or intensive pronoun in each blank.

Example   Mrs. Nosalski built the ham radio by _____.
                   Mrs. Nosalski built the ham radio by herself.

1. The land _____ is full of mystery.

2. Mr. Fallon blames _____ for the expedition's failure.

3. We _____ are making the costumes for the spring musical.

4. Laura watched _____ on the videotape of the debate competition.

5. Adam and Jeremy have learned to operate the computer by _____.

6. I always accomplish more when I study by _____.

7. President George Bush, a baseball fan, was _____ a baseball player when he was in college.

Pronouns (I)

A. Identifying Types of Pronouns

Underline the pronouns in each sentence. In the space above each pronoun, label it **P** for personal, **R** for reflexive, **I** for intensive, or **D** for demonstrative.

James Earl Carter, Jr., was elected President of the United States in 1976.

(1) People called him "Jimmy" and he himself preferred the nickname. **(2)** In his second attempt to gain the Oval Office, Carter was defeated by Ronald Reagan. **(3)** During the Carter presidency, relations between the United States and the Soviet Union declined to their lowest point in many years. **(4)** This was partly the result of the Soviet Union's invasion of Afghanistan. **(5)** In addition, during Carter's term of office, a group of Americans were held hostage in the United States Embassy in Tehran by Iranian revolutionaries; they were protesting American support for their deposed shah. The hostages were not released until Ronald Reagan was inaugurated in 1981. **(6)** Nevertheless, Jimmy Carter can congratulate himself for his important accomplishments as President. **(7)** These were in the diplomatic arena. **(8)** He helped to build diplomatic relations between China and the United States. **(9)** In addition, he helped Israel and Egypt to end their historic hostilities. **(10)** They signed the Camp David Accords.

B. Using Pronouns

Complete each sentence with the type of pronoun specified in parentheses. Write the pronoun in the blank.

1. Janet (intensive) _____ repaired the computer.

2. I took these photos; Dino took (demonstrative) _____ on the wall.

3. Here comes my bus, but where is (personal) _____?

4. The Kaufmans painted their house and garage by (reflexive) _____.

5. If you're looking for Tim and Ann, (personal) _____ left five minutes ago.

6. This seashell is from Bermuda, but (demonstrative) _____ is a local one.

7. You and I will work together, and (personal) _____ will do a great job.

8. Excuse (personal) _____ while I answer the doorbell.

9. Jason and I organized the rally (reflexive) _____.

10. I (intensive) _____ prefer the novels of Franz Kafka.

Pronouns (II)

Three other types of pronouns are described below.

Indefinite pronouns	do not refer to definite persons or things
Singular	*another, anybody, anyone, anything, each,*
	everybody, everyone, everything, much,
	neither, nobody, no one, nothing, one,
	somebody, someone, something
Plural	*both, few, many, several*
Singular or Plural	*all, any, more, most, none, some*
Interrogative pronouns	introduce questions (*Who? Whom? Whose? Which? What?*)
Relative pronouns	relate, or connect, a clause to the word or words modified (*who, whom, whose, which, that*)

A. Identifying Pronouns

Underline the indefinite, interrogative, and relative pronouns in these sentences.

1. Which of the animals is classified as a mollusk?

2. No one knows mathematics better than Mrs. Liebowitz.

3. *Les Miserables,* which has been made into a musical, was written by Victor Hugo.

4. Few of us know what careers we will pursue when we leave school.

5. Guglielmo Marconi was the person who invented radio.

6. The congressional candidates whom we saw on TV were very impressive.

7. Neither of those big budget movies did well at the box office.

8. Who was the first person to reach the North Pole?

B. Identifying Kinds of Pronouns

Identify the boldfaced pronoun in each of the following sentences by writing **indefinite, interrogative,** or **relative** in the blank.

Example   South Africa excludes **most** of its population from the political process.   **indefinite**

1. The class president, **who** just left, was extremely effective. _____

2. **Someone** offered to paint a mural on the side of the building. _____

3. **Which** of these reference works lists famous quotations? _____

4. All seven crew members of the space shuttle *Challenger* were killed in an explosion **that** stunned the world. _____

5. Martina bought some haddock, **which** she will cook for dinner. _____

6. Paul is a person whom **everyone** admires. _____

7. **Whose** is this fifty-dollar bill on the floor. _____

A. Identifying Pronouns
Underline the indefinite, interrogative, and relative pronouns in these paragraphs. Identify each pronoun by writing **IND** for indefinite, **INT** for interrogative, or **R** for relative above it.

(1) Samuel Langhorne Clemens, who wrote under the pen name Mark Twain, was born in Missouri in 1835. (2) What was his childhood in Hannibal, Missouri, like? (3) Some have said that Twain—the leader of a gang of rough-and-ready youngsters— was the model for his own creation, Tom Sawyer.

(4) The Mississippi River, which stretches for thousands of miles, formed the basis for Twain's early experiences and observations. (5) The Mississippi was a "superhighway" that carried many of the colorful "types" who were eventually depicted in Twain's writings: con men, criminals, gold-rush forty-niners, homesteaders, and others. (6) When his father died, Twain took various jobs to help support his family; several suited him, but eventually he took the job that he had prepared for in his youth: riverboat pilot.

(7) When the Civil War erupted, Twain left Missouri to join his brother who was living in Nevada. (8) Which side was Missouri on during the Civil War? (9) Missouri was a border state that stayed in the Union—even though it allowed slavery, a subject that is discussed in Mark Twain's popular novel *The Adventures of Huckleberry Finn*.

B. Using Pronouns
Write three sentences about the best trip you ever took. In each sentence, use the type of pronoun indicated in parentheses.

1. (indefinite pronoun) _____

_____

2. (interrogative pronoun) _____

_____

3. (relative pronoun) _____

_____

Blue Level, Copyright © McDougal, Littell & Company

Verbs (I)

A **verb** is a word that expresses an action, a condition, or a state of being. These are three types of verbs:

Action verbs	tell what physical or mental action someone or something is performing (*run, break, think*)
Linking verbs	link the subject of the sentence to a word in the predicate (forms of *be, feel, taste, smell, sound, look, grown, seem, appear, become, stay*)
Auxiliary or Helping verbs	make up a verb phrase when combined with a main verb (*must, might, can, may, will, could, should, would,* and forms of *be, have,* and *do*)

Identifying Types of Verbs

In the following sentences, underline each verb. Be sure to include any helping verbs. Then in the blank, write **A** if it is an action verb or **L** if it is a linking verb. Remember: the contraction *n't* is not part of the verb.

Example   The persistent buzz of the alarm clock <u>grew</u> louder.   **L**

1. Ying felt ill for several weeks. _____

2. The watery juice inside the barrel cactus saved their lives. _____

3. The Great Wall of China was a defense against the Huns. _____

4. The abacus is a helpful instrument for mathematical calculations. _____

5. Vincent van Gogh sold only one painting during his lifetime. _____

6. The whole city did, in fact, benefit from the growth of new industry. _____

7. Insurance protects against the financial consequences of injury. _____

8. China had been invaded by foreign armies several times. _____

9. The largest snakes are members of the boa family. _____

10. Cindy can't join us. _____

11. Could space exploration have advanced so rapidly without computers? _____

12. In 1910, the earth may have passed through the tail of Halley's comet. _____

13. In Kabuki theater, men dress as women, children, and animals. _____

14. She seemed energetic after the aerobic workout. _____

15. Don't you like yogurt? _____

Verbs (I)

A. Identifying Verb Phrases

In the following sentences, underline auxiliary verbs once and main verbs twice.

1. Do some lizards of Southeast Asia really glide from tree to tree?

2. Eubie Blake was still playing the piano in his ninety-ninth year.

3. Over two hundred thousand ocean-dwelling organisms have been identified.

4. "Talking" computers will aid visually impaired students and executives.

5. According to legend, the swan does not sing until just before it dies.

6. Erosion has become a major concern in the Galápagos Islands.

7. The final inning of the ball game could soon be starting.

8. Have you ever visited Niagara Falls?

9. The new club officers would have been chosen by tomorrow night.

10. You could have gone to the principal's office without me.

11. By the year 2000, the world's population will have increased dramatically.

12. We might be electing class officers tomorrow.

13. The campers should definitely have pitched their tents on higher ground.

14. The villagers had rarely, if ever, seen an airplane on the ground.

15. This species of ant may have vanished from the rain forest.

B. Using Action and Linking Verbs

Complete each of the following sentences with an appropriate action or linking verb. Then, in the blanks, identify each verb you have used by writing **A** for action or **L** for linking.

1. My father _____ an attorney. _____

2. The San Diego Zoo's natural habitats _____ real. _____

3. He _____ feverish, but I don't believe that he is seriously ill. _____

4. Nobody _____ the dictator's promises. _____

5. The American Civil War _____ in 1861. _____

6. Benny Goodman, who died in 1986, _____ a famous jazz clarinetist and band leader. _____

7. Suddenly, the enraged bear _____ at the door of its cave. _____

8. Despite her disappointment, she _____ happy. _____

9. Sheila _____ everywhere for her history notes. _____

10. The symptoms of the bubonic plague, which swept Europe during the Middle Ages, _____ gruesome. _____

Verbs (II)

An action verb can be transitive or intransitive. A **transitive verb** always takes a direct object; an **intransitive verb** does not take an object. Since they do not take direct objects, linking verbs are always intransitive. Compare these sentences:

Transitive	Jack Nicklaus **won** the tournament. (*Tournament* is the object of the verb *won*.)
Intransitive	The puppies **frolicked**. (No object follows the verb.) Everyone **arrived** safely. (*Safely* is an adverb, not an object.)

A. Identifying Transitive and Intransitive Verbs

Identify the boldfaced verb as transitive or intransitive by writing **T** or **I** in the blank.

1. The tall building **swayed** slightly in the strong wind. _____

2. Caterpillars eventually **become** butterflies. _____

3. The principal **distributed** attendance prizes at the awards assembly. _____

4. Who **knows** the solution to the problem? _____

5. The audience **applauded** loudly at the end of the play. _____

6. Acid rain **caused** the deterioration of the outdoor statuary. _____

7. Not one student **answered** the question correctly. _____

8. The circus train **arrived** in town early in the morning. _____

B. Using Transitive and Intransitive Verbs

Use a form of each of the verbs listed below in two sentences, first as an intransitive verb and then as a transitive verb.

Example	see (intransitive)	**Fred sees well with his new bifocals.**
	(transitive)	**Have you seen our new science lab?**

1. play: (intransitive) _____

   (transitive) _____

2. dance: (intransitive) _____

   (transitive) _____

3. move: (intransitive) _____

   (transitive) _____

4. grow: (intransitive) _____

   (transitive) _____

Verbs (II)

A. Identifying Transitive and Intransitive Verbs

Identify the boldfaced verbs in the following sentences by writing **T** for transitive and **I** for intransitive in the blanks. If the verb is transitive, draw a line under the direct object.

1. Frank Lloyd Wright *was* a very important American architect. _____

2. He *lived* from 1867 to 1959. _____

3. Wright *studied* engineering for a while at the University of Wisconsin. _____

4. Later, he *moved* to Chicago to work as a draftsman for a well-known architect. _____

5. Wright *designed* significant public and private structures during his career. _____

6. In 1932, Wright *founded* the Taliesin Fellowship, which had its summer residence in Wisconsin and a winter home in Arizona. _____

7. The Taliesin Fellowship *provides* a work-study program for architecture students. _____

8. Wright *became* very well known in the United States and abroad. _____

9. Two of his famous structures *are* the Guggenheim Museum, an art museum in New York City, and the civic center in Marin County, California. _____

10. He also *planned* the Imperial Hotel complex in Tokyo. _____

11. One of Wright's goals, providing low-cost housing, *promoted* the development of structures made from precast concrete blocks. _____

12. Wright's autobiography *describes* his architectural philosophy. _____

B. Using Transitive and Intransitive Verbs

Use the following verbs or verb phrases to write eight sentences. Make four of the verbs you use transitive and four of them intransitive.

has   become   lost   discovered   swam   are   winning   look   develop   spread

1. (transitive) _____

2. (transitive) _____

3. (transitive) _____

4. (transitive) _____

5. (intransitive) _____

6. (intransitive) _____

7. (intransitive) _____

8. (intransitive) _____

Adjectives

An **adjective** is a word that modifies a noun or a pronoun. An adjective answers one of the following questions: *Which one? What kind? How many? How much?* A **proper adjective,** such as *American* or *English,* is formed from a proper noun and is always capitalized. A **predicate adjective** follows a linking verb and modifies the subject of the sentence. The articles *a, an,* and *the* are also adjectives.

A. Identifying Adjectives

Underline each adjective once and the word that it modifies twice in each of the following sentences. Do not underline the articles.

1. The graves of the Incas of Peru often contained golden objects.

2. Several small sharks circled in the shallow water.

3. Ada reported the information to the editors in the busy newsroom.

4. The pyramids of Giza were among the seven wonders of the ancient world.

5. Most people speculate hopefully about the future.

6. A major earthquake devastated the region.

7. The posters were designed by a brilliant artist named Valdez.

8. The concerned ecologist wanted to preserve the habitat of the rare birds.

9. Black bear sometimes steal supplies from careless campers.

10. David Buick built an early model automobile.

B. Identifying Proper and Predicate Adjectives

Underline the adjective once and the word that it modifies twice in each of the following sentences. If the adjective is a proper adjective, write **proper** in the blank. If the adjective is a predicate adjective, write **predicate** in the blank.

Example   The water feels chilly.   **predicate**

1. The Chinese leader appeared briefly at the parade.   _____

2. Stories by O. Henry are often sentimental.   _____

3. The chicken was delicious.   _____

4. The speech in favor of the referendum seemed effective.   _____

5. Tourists enjoy riding in Venetian gondolas.   _____

6. The temperature remained steady throughout the week.   _____

7. Ingrid teaches a class in Swedish gymnastics.   _____

8. Before the twins arrived, life at camp had been carefree.   _____

9. Spices are useful for improving the taste of food.   _____

10. The museum is currently exhibiting Italian sculpture.   _____

Adjectives

A. Identifying Proper and Predicate Adjectives

Underline each adjective once and the word that it modifies twice. If the adjective is a proper adjective, write **proper** in the blank. If it is a predicate adjective, write **predicate** in the blank.

1. People discovered thousands of years ago that wool can be protective. _____

2. Our Asian ancestors "picked" wool that had caught on branches. _____

3. The surface of wool is resistant to water. _____

4. The fibers of its interior are absorbent. _____

5. Scottish shepherds used to rinse woolens with water before wearing them. _____

6. The clothes were then less permeable by air. _____

7. Maine fishers, therefore, wear mittens of wool. _____

8. Irish fishers wore sweaters of wool that had patterns from their villages. _____

9. Felt, wool that had been matted, also proved useful long ago. _____

10. Asian nomads made clothing and tents of felt. _____

11. In Rome breastplates made of felt were popular with soldiers. _____

12. Turkish yurts were dwellings constructed from willow and felt. _____

B. Using Adjectives

Fill in the blanks with one or more adjectives to improve the descriptions of the mystery-story characters presented below.

The butler has gray, wavy hair and wears a faded jacket with a button missing. Lady Margery wears expensive jewelry and has a resonant voice. **(1)** Lord James wears suits and scarves, and he is surprisingly _____. Penelope walks with tiny steps and wears her auburn hair in tight curls. **(2)** The maid wears a _____ uniform, and she speaks in a _____ voice. Mrs. Lunt has penetrating brown eyes and walks with an ebony cane. **(3)** Mr. Lunt is old, with _____ skin. **(4)** The visitor from the United States has _____ hair, _____ eyes, and a _____ laugh. Agatha has a mischievous smile, a messy appearance, and tangled hair. **(5)** Dr. Wooster seems quite _____.

Blue Level, Copyright © McDougal, Littell & Company

Adverbs

An **adverb** is a word that modifies a verb, an adjective, or another adverb. Adverbs answer the question *Where? When? How?* or *To what extent?* Many adverbs are formed by adding *-ly* to an adjective: *cheerful, cheerfully*. Other common adverbs include *no, not, never*, and time words such as *soon, later*, and *often*.

A. Identifying Adverbs

Underline the adverb once and the word that it modifies twice in each of the following sentences.

1. The TV director immediately replayed the footage of the field goal.

2. Kent seemed absolutely certain about the outcome of the test.

3. Robots perform many industrial tasks daily.

4. Isadora Duncan often interpreted human experience through dance.

5. Wait for us outside on the library steps.

6. Many psychiatrists today use the ink-blot test for personality analysis.

7. The Mediterranean Sea can look quite green from a distance.

8. A warm fire beckoned the travelers inside.

9. Can meteorologists predict weather accurately?

10. Sarah worked hard for her promotion to assistant manager.

B. Identifying Uses of Adverbs

Adverbs in the following sentences are boldfaced. On the line, write the word that each adverb modifies. Label the modified word **verb**, **adjective**, or **adverb**.

Example   Sky diving is an *incredibly* dangerous hobby.
dangerous; adjective

1. That jazz musician talked *too* long about music theory._____

2. Engineering students *regularly* use calculators. _____

3. Laura's proficiency in French has increased *steadily* with practice. _____

4. Agatha Christie is a *very* popular author of mystery stories. _____

5. Jerry spotted his error *instantly* and stopped. _____

6. The lake became *almost* dry during the long drought._____

7. Neil Armstrong took the *very* first steps on the lunar surface. _____

8. Ernie worked *extremely* hard on his stamp collection._____

9. A crowd gathered *early* at the ticket booth. _____

10. It was a *rather* difficult time for the whole team. _____

Adverbs

A. Identifying Adverbs

Study the boldfaced adverb in each sentence below. Then, on the line, write the word each adverb modifies and the question the adverb answers: **where? how? when? to what extent?**

> **Example**   Mara **cautiously** entered the ice rink. **entered; how?**

1. As a diplomat, Ben Franklin was *particularly* successful. _____

2. Mario *patiently* demonstrated the complicated macramé knot. _____

3. My cousins returned to Canada *yesterday.* _____

4. Luisa now speaks English *fluently.* _____

5. Bill is *quite* sure that his information is accurate. _____

6. Larry *secretly* longed to be a hero in the days of King Arthur. _____

7. Tim pedaled *more* slowly as he approached the intersection. _____

8. The woman gazed *wistfully* out the window. _____

9. Mr. Spellman left his laundry *outside* in the rain. _____

10. Nina *always* works at the gas station after school. _____

B. Using Adverbs

This paragraph is a first-person account of an ice storm. The account could be improved by the addition of adverbs. On the lines below, rewrite each numbered sentence. Include an adverb that modifies the boldfaced verb.

> The storm struck unexpectedly. One moment, white clouds floated deceptively overhead. The next moment, they broke. **(1)** I watched hailstones *drop*. In a few seconds, there was a thick coating of ice on streets and sidewalks. **(2)** Like animals from an ice forest, parked cars *crouched.* There was only the drumming of the hail for several minutes. Then a noise burst the air. **(3)** The air *crackled* as a power line leaned on a fence. **(4)** Police officers *drove* along the icy street in response to accident calls. **(5)** I *realized* that my neighborhood might belong on another planet, an ice planet. All landmarks seemed carved out of ice.

1. _____

2. _____

3. _____

4. _____

5. _____

Prepositions

A **preposition** is a word that is used to show the relationship between a noun or a pronoun and another word in a sentence. A preposition and its object, plus any modifiers the object may have, form a **prepositional phrase.** Read the examples below.

Common Prepositions

about	by	on, onto
across	during	through
after	for	to
among	from	toward
at	in, into	under
behind	of	with

Common Compound Prepositions

according to	in addition to
because of	out of
on account of	instead of
aside from	in place of
out of	prior to

A. Identifying Prepositions

Underline the prepositions and compound prepositions in the following sentences.

1. During his childhood, Walt Whitman lived in Brooklyn, New York.

2. After the concert, everyone praised the conductor.

3. Many insects hear with their hair.

4. During study hall, I read some poetry by Mari Evans.

5. A porcupine uses its sharp quills for protection.

6. The giraffe's long neck has only seven bones in it.

7. Maria Tallchief wrote a book about ballet.

8. Because of bad weather the school picnic was canceled.

9. Instead of New York, the immigrants entered through San Francisco.

10. The language department offers Latin and Spanish in addition to French.

B. Identifying Prepositions and Objects

Underline the prepositional phrase or phrases in each of the following sentences. Label each preposition **P** and each object of the preposition **OP**.

```
                            P     OP
Example     I found the bracelet in the lobby.
```

1. Nephrite and jadeite are two kinds of jade.

2. During the night, the wind destroyed our elm tree.

3. Many carpets are woven from camel hair.

4. Elephants in the region are protected.

5. The race car crashed through the wall and flipped onto its side.

6. The umpire stands behind the catcher.

7. Sonar detects submarines and other objects under water.

8. Louis Pasteur discovered that microbes can be filled by heat.

9. Prior to 1950, few homes in America had television sets.

10. Mount Fuji, Japan's highest mountain, is a holy place according to the Shinto religion.

Prepositions

A. Identifying Prepositional Phrases

Underline the propositional phrases in the following sentences. Some of the sentences contain more than one prepositional phrase.

1. Plenty of rest, in addition to a healthful diet, is essential to maintain fitness.
2. *Georgia* is also the name of a republic in the Soviet Union.
3. My grandparents live across the river, in Mexico.
4. Our basketball team will play against yours in the playoffs.
5. The mechanic slid beneath the car and checked the oil pan.
6. Bethany identified ten varieties of flowers along the river.
7. Amanda waited through the long night at the hospital.
8. Phil jumped from the porch onto the grass.
9. The coach said, "Play the game according to the new rules."
10. Have you seen the Impressionist exhibit at the art museum?
11. The alert forest ranger noticed a cloud of smoke on the horizon.
12. Enrique planted marigolds among the tomato plants.
13. By mistake the shipment went to India instead of Japan.
14. We've lived behind the bakery for ten years.
15. In spite of bad weather, the climbers continued their ascent toward the summit.

B. Using Prepositions

The following is a first-person account of a child, a dog, and a new catcher's mitt. Fill in the blanks in the numbered sentences with appropriate prepositions.

I was playing with my catcher's mitt on the back steps. I was pounding the ball into the palm of my mitt, ignoring Bing, whose ball it was. (Bing is the dog next door.) Suddenly, Bing grabbed for his ball, but he grabbed my new mitt instead and tore into the alley. **(1)** I chased him _____ the alley. Bing ran behind the A-1 Finest Foods store. Boxes were piled at the back door. **(2)** I saw Bing's tail disappearing _____ the boxes and dived after him. **(3)** As I lay _____ the heap of boxes, I saw Bing flying _____ the fence. "Come back!" I wailed furiously. "Bring back my mitt!" **(4)** Then I heard a panting _____ my ear. **(5)** Bing was standing _____ me, a wet, drooled-over, limp mitt _____ his mouth. He laid it beside me and waited to play catch. Ugh!

What are you going to do?

Conjunctions

A **conjunction** is a word that connects words or groups of words. The three kinds of conjunctions are described below.

Coordinating conjunctions	connect words or groups of words that have the same function in a sentence (*and, but, or, for, yet*)
Correlative conjunctions	are similar to coordinating conjunctions but are always used in pairs (*not only . . . but also; either . . . or; neither . . . nor; both . . . and*)
Subordinating conjunctions	introduce subordinate clauses— clauses that cannot stand alone (*whenever, when, although, because, since, so that, unless, even though, if*)

Conjunctive adverbs, such as *also, however, consequently, nevertheless,* and *therefore,* connect independent clauses—clauses that can stand alone in a sentence.

Identifying Conjunctions

Underline the conjunctions and the conjunctive adverbs in the following sentences.

1. Insects do not have lungs; instead, they breathe through tiny holes in their bodies.
2. Professional athletes are well paid, but they usually retire when they are relatively young.
3. Although they were both writers of renown, neither Mark Twain nor Robert Frost ever received a Nobel Prize.
4. The dodo bird is extinct; however, other flightless birds do exist.
5. The debating team chose both Darryl and Kate to represent them in the finals.
6. Mr. Sanchez wants us to turn in our reports by Friday so that he can read them over the weekend.
7. The tailless Manx cat is an unusual breed; still, it acts like other cats.
8. People have become more aware of the plight of the homeless because the media have been covering the issue very intensely lately.
9. Ms. Snyder said we could borrow her bicycle whenever we wanted to.
10. English is now one of the most widely spoken languages in the world; however, at one time it was not even the official language of England.
11. Unless it rains, we'll pick you up at six o'clock sharp.
12. They spoke either French or Spanish the whole day.
13. Stavros is not only class president but also captain of the swimming team.
14. Sandy loves to sail, yet he can't swim very well.
15. Since the lawn was fertilized in the fall, it will grow well in the spring.

Conjunctions

A. Identifying Conjunctions
Underline the conjunctions and the conjunctive adverbs.

1. Either Ali or James will have the lead in the junior-class play.
2. Some common plants are poisonous; therefore, they should be kept away from small children.
3. Both Winston Churchill and Albert Einstein were poor students.
4. That car is ten years old; however, it still runs smoothly.
5. Since Jason has an after-school job, he can't try out for the tennis team.
6. Susan plans to take a short vacation if she can get some time off.
7. Neither radio nor television offered any good programs last night.
8. Paul Revere was not only a silversmith but also a dentist.

B. Using Conjunctions
Underline the conjunctions and the conjunctive adverbs in the following sentences. Then in the blanks, identify these words by writing **coordinating, correlative, subordinating,** or **conjunctive adverb.**

Example   <u>Both</u> Penny <u>and</u> Antonio work on the school paper.

correlative

1. Picasso was a famous painter; also, he was a sculptor. _____

2. Neither the president nor the vice president will attend. _____

3. There was a great deal of discussion, yet nothing was decided. _____

4. I hope we'll have a class party when school is over in June. _____

5. Tanya will take either mechanical drawing or art next semester. _____

6. Snow crystals are all different, but each has six points. _____

7. The lizard detached its tail; consequently, it escaped capture. _____

8. The candidate was not only articulate but also well informed. _____

9. Even though the United States is a comparatively young country, it has the oldest written constitution in the world. _____

10. Both Illinois and Michigan are named for Native American peoples. _____

11. Mr. Wilson has just moved to the state; therefore, he can't vote yet. _____

12. Our class plans to invite Senator Yamamoto to speak to us because we want to know more about how our state government works. _____

Interjections

An **interjection** is a word or group of words that expresses feeling or emotion. An interjection may precede a sentence or appear within a sentence. An interjection that precedes a sentence is followed by an exclamation point or a comma. An interjection within a sentence is set off by commas.

A. Identifying Interjections

Underline the interjection in each of the following sentences.

1. Hah! I knew you didn't have a ten-foot crocodile in your basement.

2. Wow! My short story won first prize!

3. The mail carrier shouted to me, "Hey, is that your dog?"

4. Oh, what a day to be caught in a snowstorm!

5. There is no one else, alas, who can help me write this poem.

6. Ugh! Look at this disgusting mess!

7. Aha! So that's where you keep your pet mouse.

8. After lifting the boxes, Tom said, "Whew! What did you put in these?"

B. Using Interjections

Rewrite each of the following sentences, adding an interjection at the beginning.

Example   That is a beautiful sweater.
Wow! That is a beautiful sweater.

1. What do you think we should do?

   _____

2. Who told you to use my locker?

   _____

3. It's just too hot to practice today.

   _____

4. There are no more free concert tickets.

   _____

5. I just spilled paint on my new shoes.

   _____

6. Who locked the door to the gym?

   _____

7. I think that milk is sour.

   _____

Interjections

A. Identifying Interjections
Underline the interjections in the following passage from *Alice in Wonderland* by Lewis Carroll.

(1) "Oh, I beg your pardon!" cried Alice. . . . "I quite forgot you didn't like cats."

"Not like cats!" cried the Mouse in a shrill, passionate voice. "Would *you* like cats, if you were me?"

(2) "Well, perhaps not," said Alice. . . . "And yet I wish I could show you our cat Dinah. . . . She is such a dear quiet thing. . . . (3) She sits purring so nicely by the fire, licking her paws and washing her face . . . and she's such a capital one for catching mice—oh, I beg your pardon!" cried Alice again. . . . "We won't talk about her any more if you'd rather not."

(4) "We, indeed!" cried the Mouse, . . . trembling down to the end of his tail. . . .

(5) "Are you fond of dogs?" [asked Alice.] "There is such a nice little dog near our house. . . . A little bright-eyed terrier, you know, with oh, such long curly brown hair. . . . (6) It belongs to a farmer [who] says it's so useful, it's worth a hundred pounds! He says it kills all the rats and—oh, dear!" cried Alice in a sorrowful tone. . . .

B. Using Interjections in Writing
Write a dialogue between two persons. Use a variety of interjections in the dialogue. Draft it on a separate sheet of paper and write the final version on the lines below. Underline the interjections.

_____

_____

_____

_____

_____

_____

_____

_____

_____

The Sentence

A **sentence** is a group of words that expresses a complete thought. A sentence can make statements, ask questions, give commands, or show strong feelings. When part of the idea is missing from a sentence, the group of words is a **sentence fragment.**

Sentence Fragment	Waiting in the wings.
Sentence	We were waiting in the wings.

A. Identifying Sentences

Identify the sentences and sentence fragments from among these group of words. Write **S** for a complete sentence and **F** for a sentence fragment.

1. Some snakes have fangs that can inject poison. _____

2. After I mixed the ingredients. _____

3. *The Lady of Shalott,* a poem by Alfred, Lord Tennyson. _____

4. What percentage of travelers use telephone credit cards? _____

5. A computer designed the seats, doors, and windows of this plane. _____

6. What is grown in Kansas? _____

7. The huge trucks rolling along the nation's highways all night long. _____

8. Looking over a four-leaf clover. _____

9. At least her heart is in the right place. _____

10. Only John is here. _____

B. Writing Complete Sentences

Write a complete sentence using each of the following groups of words.

1. On the western shore of Lake Michigan, Milwaukee, Wisconsin. _____

_____

2. A life preserver when you go sailing. _____

_____

3. The islands of the Hawaiian chain. _____

_____

4. Long tradition of superb bronze sculpture from Benin, West Africa. _____

_____

5. The study of Navajo sand paintings. _____

_____

A. Using the Sentence

The following paragraph contains both sentences and sentence fragments. Write the number of each sentence fragment. Then rewrite the fragment as a complete sentence, combining fragments and sentences as necessary.

(1) With 700 million people, India has the second largest population in the world. (2) Three times that of the United States. (3) India's huge population is matched only by its diversity. (4) For example, consider the matters of language and religion. (5) Two official languages. (6) English and Hindi. (7) At least thirteen others also spoken, excluding hundreds of dialects. (8) Five major religious groups: Hindus, Muslims, Christians, Buddhists, and Jainists. (9) Each group celebrates its own holidays. (10) Imagine an Indian calendar. (11) Number of holidays on it. (12) Such diversity has a bonus. (13) Though. (14) School children and office workers get many holidays.

_____

_____

_____

_____

_____

_____

_____

B. Writing Complete Sentences

Write complete sentences to form a paragraph from the sentence fragments below.

1. Mother Teresa born in Yugoslavia. Parents Albanian.

2. Became missionary nun. Learned health care. Wanted to help the sick.

3. Went to India. Lived and worked in Calcutta. Poor and sick cared for.

4. Life of love. Forgotten people of India. Compassion and strength.

_____

_____

_____

_____

_____

_____

Kinds of Sentences

A sentence may be classified according to the purpose it serves. A **declarative sentence** expresses a statement of fact, wish, intent, or feeling and ends with a period. An **interrogative sentence** asks a question and ends with a question mark. An **imperative sentence** gives a command, request, or direction. It usually ends with a period but may end with an exclamation point if the command is strong. An **exclamatory sentence** expresses strong feelings and always ends with an exclamation point.

A. Identifying Kinds of Sentences

In the blank, identify each sentence as **DEC** for declarative, **INT** for interrogative, **IMP** for imperative, or **EXCL** for exclamatory.

1. First, buy the stamp; then, mail the letter   _____

2. Was an unknown type of dinosaur recently unearthed in England   _____

3. What an amazing story that was   _____

4. Please finish this job application at home   _____

5. Some artists who paint what they imagine or dream are called surrealists   _____

6. Did you know that the earth's largest animals are vegetarians   _____

7. Trees get 90 percent of their nutrients from the air   _____

8. Bring your racket so we can play tennis   _____

9. The boat is sinking   _____

10. Why are there more female than male millionaires in the United States   _____

B. Using Different Kinds of Sentences

In the blank on the right, identify each sentence as **DEC** for declarative, **INT** for interrogative, **IMP** for imperative, or **EXCL** for exclamatory. On the line below, write a new sentence of the kind indicated in parentheses, using the same subject and verb. You may have to add or delete words and change word order.

1. That quarterback really throws long passes   _____

   (interrogative) _____

2. Did you look at that unusual sports car   _____

   (imperative) _____

3. Is the Amazon the longest river in the world   _____

   (declarative) _____

4. Pick the apples when they are ripe   _____

   (interrogative) _____

Kinds of Sentences

A. Identifying Kinds of Sentences

In the blank, identify each sentence as **DEC** for declarative, **INT** for interrogative, **IMP** for imperative, or **EXCL** for exclamatory. Insert the appropriate end mark at the end of each sentence.

1. How we all laughed when Ben did an imitation of Steve Martin _____

2. Did you attend last night's Pops concert on the Esplanade _____

3. Just add a little Italian dressing to my salad, please _____

4. Transcendentalism was a literary movement centered in New England during the 1840's _____

5. How does an allegory differ from a simile and a metaphor _____

6. Turn left at the next set of lights _____

7. Will I ever be happy when we get an air conditioner _____

8. The Appalachian Trail extends from Maine down to Georgia. _____

B. Using Different Kinds of Sentences in Writing

Rewrite the description below to include dialogue as well as description. In your revision, use each of the four kinds of sentences (declarative, interrogative, exclamatory, and imperative) at least once. Drop or add words as necessary.

Like a stuck record, the barker kept yelling for "la-deez" and "gen-tul-men" to step right up. Todd asked, almost out loud, if he was talking to him. Then the human loudspeaker confirmed his thoughts by telling him how strong he looked. He even suggested that Todd was Paul Bunyan in disguise. Todd let out an exclamation of surprise and said why not give it a try. Then he elbowed forward and grasped the sledgehammer.

_____

_____

_____

_____

_____

_____

_____

_____

Complete Subjects and Predicates

A sentence has two parts: a complete subject and a complete predicate. The **complete subject** includes all the words that identify the person, place, thing, or idea that the sentence is about. The **complete predicate** includes all the words that tell what the subject did or what happened to the subject.

Complete Subject	Complete Predicate
A girl in my government class /	worked for our state senator last summer.
Charles Dickens /	published *A Tale of Two Cities* in 1859.

A. Identifying Complete Subjects and Predicates

Underline the complete subject once and the complete predicate twice in each of the following sentences.

1. Ancient Romans were very superstitious.

2. The sting of the jellyfish's tentacles paralyzes its prey.

3. England's crown jewels are kept in the Tower of London.

4. Danali, also known as Mount McKinley, is the highest peak in North America.

5. Bald eagles are considered an endangered species.

B. Using Complete Subjects and Predicates

In the blank, identify each sentence fragment as **CS** for complete subject or **CP** for complete predicate. Then combine fragments to make three logical, complete sentences on the lines provided below.

1. all students of the remedial reading program _____

2. flew past us _____

3. tigers, lions, and leopards in zoos _____

4. a beautiful great blue heron _____

5. need large cages or extensive fenced areas _____

6. have made great progress _____

7. the slow-moving automobile _____

8. _____

   _____

9. _____

   _____

10. _____

    _____

Complete Subjects and Predicates

A. Using Complete Subjects and Predicates

Write eight logical sentences on the lines below by combining complete subjects and complete predicates from the following lists.

Complete Subjects	Complete Predicates
1. The man in the moon	crossed the Atlantic in 1907
2. Two oarsmen	pioneered manned spacecraft
3. A Soviet astronaut	could spoil our outdoor plans
4. The desert	fluctuates with the economy
5. Our high school principal	are needed by the year 2000
6. The stock market	blooms after heavy rain
7. New sources of energy	dedicated our new gymnasium
8. Bad weather	is a character from folk tales
9. Several tall oak trees	was based on a best-selling novel
10. The popular new film	towered above the cabin

1. _____

2. _____

3. _____

4. _____

5. _____

6. _____

7. _____

8. _____

9. _____

10. _____

B. Using Complete Subjects and Predicates in Writing

Write a descriptive paragraph about food, a sport, or a hobby. Draft your paragraph on a separate page and write the final version on the lines below. Underline the complete subjects once and the complete predicates twice.

_____

_____

_____

_____

_____

_____

_____

Simple Subjects and Predicates

The **simple subject** is the key word or words in the complete subject. It does not include modifiers. To find the simple subject, ask *who* or *what* before the verb. A simple subject made of two or more key words is a **compound subject.** The parts of a compound subject are joined by a conjunction.

Simple Subject	*Tom* works hard.
Compound Subject	*Tom* and *Alex* work hard.

The **simple predicate,** also called the **verb,** is the key word or words in the complete predicate. The verb may be a phrase: *had seen, should have seen, was singing, had been singing.* The words making up the verb phrase may be interrupted by a modifier, which is not part of the verb. A **compound verb** is made up of two or more verbs or verb phrases joined by a conjunction.

Verb	Eileen *will arrive* by eight o'clock.
Compound Verb	Eileen *will arrive* or *call* by eight o'clock.

A. Identifying Simple Subjects and Verbs
Underline the simple subject once and the verb twice in each sentence.

1. The captivated audience gave the singer a standing ovation.
2. Maria, our cheerleading captain, shouted above the crowd's noise.
3. Hawaii, the fiftieth state, joined the Union in 1959.
4. Starfish can regenerate broken limbs.
5. Both of us plan to participate in the competition.
6. Our porch is the coolest part of our house.
7. Under the door crept the mouse.
8. This intricately carved lattice screen had been made in India.
9. The small warbler with colorful plumage was singing the entire morning.
10. My grandmother's silver teapot had once been the property of a famous collector.

B. Identifying Compound Subjects and Verbs
Underline each compound subject once and each compound verb twice. Some sentences do not have both a compound subject and a compound verb.

1. The unicorn, the phoenix, and the centaur are mythological animals.
2. Julia Child writes cookbooks and has her own television show.
3. Judy Blume and Isaac Asimov write books for young adults.
4. In the winter, Hope and Marlene ski and ice-skate.
5. Santa Fe and Tucson are historic cities in the Southwest.
6. The Old English sheepdog and the collie are classified as herding dogs.
7. On Sunday afternoon we will swim in the lake or hike around it.
8. The director and the producer met today and signed the film contract.
9. Pioneers crossed the Rocky Mountains and settled the West.
10. Laurel and Hardy starred in silent film comedies.

Simple Subjects and Predicates

A. Identifying Subjects and Verbs
Underline the simple or compound subject once and the verb twice in each sentence below.

1. Robin washed and waxed the new sports car.
2. The police detectives and firefighters are at the scene of the fire.
3. The Royal Ballet came to our city and danced three programs.
4. Guinea-Bissau, Mozambique, and Angola once were Portuguese colonies.
5. *Mrs. Frisby and the Rats of NIMH* grips both the reader's imagination and conscience.
6. From 1876 to 1890, an estimated 200,000 Chinese laborers entered West Coast ports.

B. Using Compound Subjects and Verbs
Combine the sentence pairs to form the sentence part indicated in parentheses. Use the conjunction—*and, or, nor,* or *but*—that makes the most sense.

1. The Saint Bernard is now a beloved pet. Once it was mainly a work dog. (compound predicate) _____

_____

2. Its ancestors were bred by Swiss monks. They were named after their monastery. (compound predicate) _____

_____

3. In the Swiss Alps, blinding snowstorms can jeopardize travelers and isolate villages. So do deadly avalanches. (compound and compound predicate) _____

_____

4. Folktales describe this powerful dog's rescue feats. Legends describe them. (compound subject) _____

_____

5. Storms did not keep this rugged rescuer from its job. Neither did avalanches. (compound subject) _____

_____

Unusually Placed Subjects

In most sentences, the subject comes before the verb. However, in **inverted sentences,** a verb or part of a verb phrase is positioned before the subject. The three most common types of inverted sentences are questions, sentences beginning with *there* and here, and sentences inverted for emphasis. In the sentences below, subjects are underlined once and verbs twice.

Question	Have you been at school?
There/Here . . .	There are twenty students.
Emphasis	At the door stood her mother.

In **imperative sentences** the subject is often not expressed, but *you* is always understood to be the subject.

> *(You)* Answer the phone.

A. Identifying Unusually Placed Subjects

In the blank, write the simple subject of each of the following sentences.

1. With the damp, humid weather came mildew. _____

2. How much does sugar contribute to tooth decay? _____

3. Is Hawaii the most southerly state of this country? _____

4. Stop! _____

5. Under my bed were my missing keys. _____

6. Answer my question. _____

7. From somewhere in the back row came a burst of laughter. _____

8. There is an old campsite in the woods.

B. Using Unusually Placed Subjects

Rewrite these sentences as inverted or imperative sentences.

1. Today's mail is over there. _____

2. He will go to sleep soon. _____

3. Talent scouts sat in the audience. _____

4. I wonder where Lucy is. _____

5. I'm asking you to help me. _____

6. That sentry stands there every day. _____

7. Few pandas live in the wild. _____

8. You will get me a ticket. _____

Unusually Placed Subjects

A. Using Unusually Placed Subjects

Rewrite each of the following sentences as an inverted or imperative sentence. Then underline each subject once and each verb twice.

1. My brand new bike lay there in the mud. _____

_____

2. The tax forms are here. _____

3. Seven spelling errors are in your essay. _____

_____

4. You must decide now. _____

5. The bells of Aberdovey chime from beneath the sea. _____

_____

6. My sister is moving to college. _____

7. You are to speak for the class. _____

8. Tourists were gathering on the dock. _____

B. Writing with Unusually Placed Subjects

On the lines provided, rewrite the following paragraph, revising it by adding at least two inverted sentences.

> You may wonder why we don't see the duck-billed platypus in zoos more often. What are the reasons? By examining the habits of the platypus, we should find some answers. First, the animal is nocturnal. Its appetite is voracious. Moreover, the platypus's riverbank burrow is almost impossible to locate or probe. Finally, like the modest panda and gorilla, it dislikes reproducing in captivity.

_____

_____

_____

_____

_____

_____

Complements

A **complement** is a word or a group of words that completes the meaning of a verb. There are four kinds of complements: direct objects, indirect objects, objective complements, and subject complements.

A **direct object**—a word or group of words that receives the action of a verb—answers the question *What?* or *Whom?* about the verb. A direct object may be compound.

>   Penny likes *roses* but not *nasturtiums*.

An **indirect object**—a word or group of words that tells *to whom* or *for whom* the action of the verb is being performed—always comes before the direct object.

>   I shall give my *dog* a bath today.

An **objective complement**—a word or group of words that follows a direct object and renames or describes that object—may be a noun or an adjective.

>   Everyone considers Polly a *leader*.   We consider the plan *realistic*.

A **subject complement** follows a linking verb and renames or describes the subject. It may be a **predicate nominative**—a noun or a pronoun that names or identifies the subject; or it may be a **predicate adjective**—an adjective that modifies the subject. Both kinds of subject complements may be a compound.

>   Olga is a *lawyer*. (predicate nominative)
>   Ben seems *eager* and *enthusiastic*. (predicate adjectives)

Identifying Complements

Underline each complement in the sentences below. Above each complement write **DO** for direct object, **IO** for indirect object, **OC** for object complement, **PN** for predicate nominative, or **PA** for predicate adjective.

1. The pyramid builders of Egypt built their kings magnificent tombs.

2. Birds become unusually quiet just before a storm.

3. Ueuecoyotl, meaning "old, old coyote," was a god of ancient Mexico.

4. Their candidate promised them either a new sports arena or a community theater.

5. People nicknamed General Charles de Gaulle "Tall Asparagus."

6. An anonymous donor gave the school a gymnasium and an Olympic-sized pool.

7. Our principal sent us and our parents letters of congratulation.

8. The pen names of Charlotte, Emily, and Anne Brontë were Currer, Ellis, and

   Acton Bell.

9. The main basis of animal classification is not geographic but developmental.

10. The tea tax of 1773 made American colonists furious and revolution almost

    certain.

Complements

A. Identifying Complements

Underline each complement in the following sentences. Then above each complement write **DO** for direct object, **IO** for indirect object, **OC** for objective complement, **PN** for predicate nominative, or **PA** for predicate adjective.

1. The Welsh pony is a small horse that was bred for use in coal mines.

2. Vienna became justly famous for its richly decorated porcelain and pastries.

3. Japan calls its deciduous cypress tree "the umbrella pine."

4. The first jet engine brought Frank Whittle fame.

5. The judges named Steve the "Rookie of the Year" in soccer.

6. The Xhosa language of South Africa contains three different click sounds.

7. Villagers of New Guinea and West Africa grow yams for a staple food.

8. The jury found him guilty but recommended a sentence of community service.

9. Dick Whittington and his cat are much-loved English folk heroes.

10. Mr. Ortega gave us a surprise quiz in trigonometry yesterday.

B. Identifying Complements in Writing

Underline all complements in this paragraph. Then above each complement write **DO** for direct object, **IO** for indirect object, **OC** for objective complement, **PN** for predicate nominative, or **PA** for predicate adjective.

(1) In variety and quantity, insects far outnumber other animals. (2) Scientists have named the largest group of insects *Coleoptera*. (3) Members of the coleopteran order are sheath-winged and usually plant-eating. (4) Many are serious pests. (5) One of the worst of these is the snout beetle. (6) This family of beetles includes many subfamilies of weevils. (7) Four hundred species infest the British Isles, and more than twenty-five hundred plague North America. (8) With their rostrum, or snout, weevils bore life-sapping holes into plants. (9) They cause farmers significant financial loss. (10) Various species render selected grains, cotton, nuts, trees, fruits, and their byproducts unmarketable. (11) These pests seem unstoppable; they sometimes follow cereals and flours from the fields onto kitchen shelves. (12) There, infested packages give offspring nourishment and unlucky consumers grief.

The Sentence Redefined

You now know that a sentence is a group of words that expresses a complete thought, contains at least one subject and one verb, and sometimes contains a complement.

A. Identifying Elements of the Sentence

In each of the following sentences, underline the simple subject once and the verb twice. Place parentheses around any complements.

1. Rocks generally fall into three classifications.

2. Those classifications are igneous, metamorphic, and sedimentary.

3. Rivers such as the Mississippi River have been depositing silt and sediments for over 500,000 years.

4. Sedimentary rocks vary in their layers of sediments; some layers are thick; others are thin.

5. Scientists consider shale and slate sedimentary rocks.

6. Some other forms are limestone, chalk, sandstone, conglomerate, and halite.

7. One can find fossils in limestone beds and in shale and slate deposits.

8. People sometimes call the sulfur and iron in shale "fool's gold."

9. Tiny shells and calcite form most chalk deposits.

10. Halite is the mineral name for table salt.

B. Writing Complete Sentences

Write a complete sentence from each group of sentence fragments. Add words as necessary.

1. *The Night Watch* by Rembrandt. A very famous painting. _____

_____

2. Elia a pseudonym for Charles Lamb. The famous essayist._____

_____

3. A letter of commendation for our mail carrier. Written by my mother. _____

_____

_____

4. My red sneakers. There on the grass. _____

_____

5. Old camp songs. While hiking at Yellowstone. _____

_____

A. Writing Complete Sentences

Rewrite each group of fragments as the kind of sentence described in parentheses.
You may have to add or delete words, change word order, or change verb tenses.

1. Stood my friend. At the top of the hill. Puzzled. Philip. (inverted) _____

_____

2. Bought Lena. Pete. Tickets for the game. (imperative) _____

_____

3. From the early movies. Famous. Laurel and Hardy comedians. Were a pair.

(declarative) _____

_____

4. Jante Sobers. Was elected town secretary and treasurer. Really. (interrogative) _____

_____

5. The powerful jet planes. High above us. Roared. (inverted) _____

_____

B. Identifying and Revising

Rewrite this paragraph to ensure that each group of words is a complete thought.

I went into the Sacramento post office. To mail a letter to my cousin in
Missouri. "Do you want first-class or express mail?" The clerk asked me. I
thought how long it used to take to deliver mail. In 1860, a letter could take
three weeks. To cross the continent. Then the Pony Express was formed.
Relays of teenagers riding fast ponies. "Express" mail took only ten days.
Travel from the railhead in Missouri to California. To cover the same
distance I chose first-class mail. I hoped for faster service than the Pony
Express.

_____

_____

_____

_____

_____

_____

_____

Prepositional Phrases

A **prepositional phrase** is a phrase that consists of a preposition, its object, and any modifiers of the object.

A prepositional phrase that modifies a noun or pronoun is an **adjective phrase.** An adjective phrase can modify a subject, direct object, indirect object, or predicate nominative. It usually tells *which one* or *what kind* about the word it modifies.

> The digital watch *on my wrist* beeped twelve. (modifies the subject *watch*)
> Longfellow wrote the poems *in this book.* (modifies the direct object *poems*)
> I gave my friend *next door* a football. (modifies the indirect object *friend*)
> It is a llama *from the Andes.* (modifies the predicate nominative *llama*)

A prepositional phrase that functions as an adverb is called an **adverb phrase.** An adverb phrase modifies a verb, an adjective, or another adverb. It tells *how, when, where,* or *to what extent* about the word it modifies.

> The vase smashed *on the floor.* (modifies the verb *smashed*)
> Otters are very skillful *at fishing.* (modifies the adjective *skillful*)
> The afterglow appears soon *after sunset.* (modifies the adverb *soon*)

Identifying Prepositional Phrases

Underline each prepositional phrase once. Underline twice the word or words that each phrase modifies.

1. Claude Monet painted three hundred pictures of the same lily pads.

2. The world's first books were made of clay and papyrus.

3. Typhoid fever is caused by a bacterium that contaminates water and milk.

4. Benjamin Franklin founded the first hospital in the United States.

5. The star closest to the earth is the sun.

6. Take the patient to the nearest hospital.

7. Mahler's *Symphony No. 3* is the longest of all symphonies.

8. Some people call Magellan's voyage the greatest sailing feat in history.

9. These peppers come from Peru.

10. During the winter months skiers can enjoy their sport.

11. Between the April showers we visited the park.

12. Scotland Yard is the headquarters of the London police force.

13. Behind the counter stood the worried clerk.

14. Our hockey team will play against your team tomorrow night.

15. The square dance is usually danced by four couples in a square formation.

16. The game of football originated in the United States.

17. The rhododendrons and the azaleas blossomed at the same time.

18. A syllogism is a form of reasoning in which a major premise and a minor premise are stated and a logical conclusion is drawn from them.

19. Many women on this reservation create silver jewelry.

20. German bombs fell on England that year.

Prepositional Phrases

A. Identifying Types of Prepositional Phrases

Underline the prepositional phrase in each of these sentences, and place parentheses around the word modified by the phrase. In the blank, identify the prepositional phrase by writing **ADJ** for adjective phrase or **ADV** for adverb phrase.

1. What is the length of the Nile River?   _____

2. The Pilgrims established a community soon after their arrival.   _____

3. The opera singer rehearses before every performance.   _____

4. The detective studied the clues with a magnifying glass.   _____

5. The size of the blue whale is enormous.   _____

6. Before 1850, people used feather-stuffed, leather golf balls.   _____

7. *Peter Pan,* an English play, was written exclusively for children.   _____

8. Raccoons are very fastidious about their food.   _____

9. The Amazon River was named after legendary Greek warriors.   _____

10. Radio astronomers study radio waves from outer space.   _____

B. Using Prepositional Phrases

Rewrite each sentence, adding a prepositional phrase to answer the question about the boldfaced word. Underline your phrase and identify it in the blank by writing **ADJ** for adjective phrase or **ADV** for adverb phrase.

1. Bill and his baseball team *played.* (Played where?)   _____

   _____

2. That *house* is ours. (Which house?)   _____

   _____

3. As you can see, Anne is a *runner.* (What kind of runner?)   _____

   _____

4. Perhaps I *could help.* (Could help when?)   _____

   _____

5. Following their graduation, the students *sang.* (Sang how?)   _____

   _____

Appositives and Appositive Phrases

An **appositive** is a noun or a pronoun that usually follows another noun or pronoun and identifies or explains it. An appositive may be compound.

> The nymph *Ariel* appears in one of Shakespeare's plays. (The appositive *Ariel* identifies the nymph.)

An **appositive phrase** consists of an appositive and its modifiers.

> The kiwi, *a bird with no tail and with tiny, useless wings,* cannot fly. (The appositive *bird* explains the subject *kiwi.* The adjective phrases *with no* tail and *with tiny, useless wings* modify the appositive *bird.*)

An appositive may be essential or nonessential. An **essential appositive** is needed to make the intended meaning of a sentence complete. A **nonessential appositive** adds extra meaning to a sentence in which the meaning is already clear and complete. Nonessential appositives are set off by commas. No commas are needed with an essential appositive.

> The economist *François Quesnay* devised some of the earliest economic models. (essential)
> Ottorino Respighi, *an Italian composer,* wrote much music. (nonessential)

A. Identifying Appositives and Appositive Phrases
Underline the appositives and appositive phrases in the following sentences.

1. The California condor, a large American vulture, lays a single egg every two years.
2. The inventor Thomas Edison patented the electric light and the phonograph.
3. Lake Superior, the world's largest body of fresh water, is turbulent.
4. Alaska, the forty-ninth state, does not have a state motto.
5. The Chinese philosopher Confucius wrote the *Analects*.
6. The encyclopedia was awarded to the valedictorian, Diana White.
7. Matisse, the French artist, designed a chapel.

B. Identifying Essential and Nonessential Appositive Phrases
Underline the appositive phrase in each of these sentences. In the blank, identify each phrase as **E** if it is essential or **NE** if it is nonessential. Add necessary commas.

1. Groucho Marx the star of many film comedies had his own television show. _____

2. Paella a Spanish dish is made from rice, chicken, and seafood. _____

3. John Steinbeck's novel *East of Eden* was written in 1952. _____

4. Suffrage the right to vote was granted to American women in 1920. _____

5. The famed football coach Knute Rockne was born in Norway. _____

6. The dodo an awkward, flightless bird has been extinct since 1700. _____

7. Sir Walter Scott the creator of *Ivanhoe* wrote historical novels. _____

8. The Roman festival Saturnalia honored the god of agriculture. _____

Appositives and Appositive Phrases

A. Identifying Essential and Nonessential Appositive Phrases

Underline the appositive phrase in each of these sentences. In the blank, identify each phrase as **E** if it is essential to the sentence, or **NE** if it is nonessential. Add necessary commas for nonessential phrases.

1. Poets have often written about the gazelle a slender antelope noted for its grace and gentleness. _____

2. Chuck Yeager the first person to fly faster than the speed of sound was a fighter pilot during World War II. _____

3. The President of the United States appointed a commission to investigate the explosion of the space shuttle *Challenger*. _____

4. The Washington Monument a marble obelisk dedicated to the memory of George Washington is the tallest structure in Washington, D.C. _____

5. The idea for the Peace Corps was originally proposed by the American philosopher William James. _____

6. One of the most spectacular of the British Crown Jewels is the Koh-i-noor a large diamond that was found in India. _____

B. Using Appositives and Appositive Phrases

One of each of the paired sentences below contains a predicate nominative. Write one sentence that combines the two sentences by using the predicate nominative as an appositive or appositive phrase.

> **Example**   John's brother is going with him. His brother is a lawyer.
> John's brother, a lawyer, is going with him.

1. Running can be an excellent conditioner. It is a popular and exhausting sport. _____

   _____

2. Jamie is in the hospital for an operation. He is a good friend of mine. _____

   _____

3. Ms. Norbert will speak at the dinner. She is president of the company. _____

   _____

4. Beatrice Webb wrote several books. She was a social reformer. _____

   _____

Infinitives and Participles

A **verbal** is a verb form that functions as a noun, an adjective, or an adverb. There are three kinds of verbals: infinitives, participles, and gerunds.

An **infinitive** is a verb form that usually begins with *to* and functions as a noun, an adjective, or an adverb. An **infinitive phrase** consists of an infinitive, its modifiers, and its complements; it may be modified by adverbs or adverb phrases.

> Athletes need *to practice daily*. (*to practice daily* is used as a noun; it functions as a direct object)
> French was easy *to learn*. (*to learn* functions as an adverb modifying *easy*)

A **participle** is a verb form that functions as an adjective. For all verbs, the **present participle** ends in *-ing*. **Past participles** usually end in *d, ed, t,* or *n*.

> *Pausing*, the pitcher surveyed the *hushed* crowd. (The present participle *pausing* modifies *pitcher*.)

A **participial phrase** consists of a participle, its modifiers, and complements. Participial phrases always function as adjectives.

> *Already warmed by the sun*, the plant began to flower. (*Already warmed by the sun* functions as an adjective modifying *plant*.)

A. Identifying Infinitives and Infinitive Phrases

Underline the infinitives and infinitive phrases in these sentences. Then identify how each is used by writing **NOUN, ADJ** (adjective), or **ADV** (adverb) in the blank.

1. In fall the ptarmigan begins to shed its brown feathers for winter white. _____

2. To be a soccer goalie requires unwavering concentration. _____

3. We made an attempt to lift the log off him. _____

4. The insurance company promised to repay everyone affected by the flood. _____

5. Dickens wrote the novel to make money. _____

6. The coach's decision to resign surprised everyone. _____

7. To help his school's publication, he joined the newspaper. _____

B. Identifying Participles and Participial Phrases

Underline the participle or participial phrase in each sentence. Use parentheses to identify the word modified in the sentence.

1. The art fair featured handcrafted jewelry.
2. Writing as quickly as possible, the students took the exam.
3. Swimming with a friend, Frances made it to the float.
4. Ed's sailboat, damaged near the stern, was unusable.
5. The boy playing the trumpet is my brother.
6. The stolen briefcase contained valuable documents.
7. The travelers saw a huge stone castle perched on the rocky cliff.

Infinitives and Participles

A. Identifying Infinitives and Infinitive Phrases

Underline each infinitive or infinitive phrase in these sentences. Then identify how each is used by writing **NOUN, ADJ** (adjective), or **ADV** (adverb) in the blank.

1. In 1893 an Indian, Mohandas K. Gandhi, decided to go to South Africa.   _____

2. Gandhi was forced to leave the whites-only compartment of the train.   _____

3. To leave the sidewalk and to walk in the street were additional orders.   _____

4. To counter these humiliations, Gandhi took up the cause of justice.   _____

5. Under his leadership, the Indian minority began to protest.   _____

6. In time, Gandhi worked to improve the harsh conditions of the Indian
   minority in South Africa.   _____

7. To remain nonviolent was the strategy he brought back to India.   _____

8. To help free India from British control, he used a method of nonviolent resistance.   _____

9. Gandhi's chief desire was to win independence for India.   _____

10. With well-publicized fasts, he dramatized the need to be nonviolent.   _____

B. Identifying Participles and Participial Phrases

Underline the participle or participial phrase in these sentences. Add parentheses to identify the word modified in the sentence.

1. Influenced by his Hindu beliefs, Gandhi felt that violence was wrong.

2. Sensing a groundswell of support from his people, he worked to promote non-violent change.

3. As he appealed to the conscience of a disturbed populace, this man hoped for an end to racial injustice.

4. Risking arrest, he disobeyed laws that he considered unfair.

5. Employing these methods, Gandhi helped India to achieve independence.

6. This inspired leader was called "Mahatma" ("Great Soul").

7. Influenced by Henry David Thoreau's *Civil Disobedience,* the Indian leader risked imprisonment to embarrass the makers of unjust laws.

8. In turn, Gandhi influenced Martin Luther King, Jr., inspiring King to employ peaceful methods to ensure rights for blacks.

9. Assassinated by political extremists, both leaders died violently.

10. Yet their proven tactics still encourage others to work for change.

Misplaced and Dangling Participles

A participle or participial phrase should be placed as close as possible to the word that it modifies. **Misplaced participles** make the meaning of a sentence unclear.

Confusing	*Baking in the oven,* John saw the pizza. (The participial phrase appears to modify *John.*)
Clear	John saw the pizza *baking in the oven.*

A **dangling participle** does not clearly modify any word in a sentence.

Confusing	*Peering through the windows,* the scenery was lovely. (Who is peering?)
Clear	*Peering through the windows,* we saw the lovely scenery.

Correcting Misplaced and Dangling Participles

Rewrite these sentences, correcting the misplaced and dangling participles.

1. Stepping on the gas, the car lurched forward. _____

_____

2. Suspected of espionage, the FBI arrested the two brothers. _____

_____

3. Using many time- and labor-saving devices, the project was finally finished. _____

_____

4. Having escaped from his captors, freedom was finally achieved. _____

_____

5. Covered with mustard and relish, I fully enjoyed the sausage. _____

_____

6. Running with all her might, the finish line was reached. _____

_____

7. Zooming through the sky, I heard the Concorde jet. _____

_____

8. Eating under the porch, I saw the squirrel. _____

_____

9. Driving through the Alps, the sunset glowed on Mont Blanc. _____

_____

10. Shattered by the war, reconciliation came slowly to the North and South. _____

_____

Misplaced and Dangling Participles

A. Identifying Misplaced Participles and Dangling Participles

Underline the misplaced or dangling participles in these sentences.

1. Sprinting for all he was worth, the record was broken by the runner.

2. Quickly gobbling up the pies, the pie-eating contest was over in three minutes.

3. Eating up the cat food, I noticed Fido.

4. Singing the national anthem, the game finally started.

5. Children stopped to pick some apples running through the orchard.

6. Adjusting the floodlights, the stage was now fully lighted.

7. Prejudiced and old-fashioned, the concert was unfavorably reviewed by the critic.

8. Cheering the home run, the ball was hit over the fence.

9. The field was irrigated by the farmer planted with sugar cane.

10. Amused by the animation, the TV cartoon made Lois laugh.

B. Correcting Misplaced and Dangling Participles in Writing

Rewrite this paragraph, correcting the misplaced or dangling participles.

(1) The streetcar is fondly remembered by many people gently swaying and quietly clicking down the track. (2) At the peak of their popularity—around 1917—trolleys transported over eleven billion people running on nearly 45,000 miles of tracks within and between cities in the United States. (3) Carrying workers to their jobs, produce to market, and even the mail, the growing U.S. economy was well served by trolleys. (4) The trolley companies encouraged people to ride the streetcar for fun building amusement parks at the end of the streetcar runs. (5) Once almost totally abandoned, many cities are now resurrecting their trolley lines.

1. _____

_____

2. _____

_____

3. _____

_____

4. _____

_____

5. _____

_____

A **gerund** is a verb form that ends in *-ing* and functions as a noun. A **gerund phrase** consists of a gerund and its modifiers and complements; it also functions as a noun.

> *Being a mountain climber* has made him unafraid of heights. (The gerund phrase is the subject of the verb *has made*.)
> Jack stopped *fixing the roof*. (The gerund phrase is the direct object of *stopped*.)
> My newest interest is *sailing*. (The gerund is a predicate nominative.)
> After *cleaning for two hours,* we thought that the house looked spotless. (The gerund phrase is the object of the preposition *after*.)
> His summer job, *painting,* really tired him out. (The gerund is an appositive.)

A. Identifying Gerunds and Gerund Phrases
Underline the gerund or gerund phrase in each sentence.

1. The firefighter received a medal for saving the child's life.
2. Ms. Norman enjoys jogging after work.
3. I remember promising Steve my old bike.
4. Standing during a two-hour train trip is not my idea of relaxation.
5. Do you like working at the supermarket?
6. Volunteering at the hospital is just one of Ray's activities.
7. Ms. Brent enjoys watching quiz shows on television.
8. Scrambling eggs over a fire is my favorite camping task.
9. Taking out the garbage is a daily job at my house.
10. The Thompsons reduced their fuel bills by installing a woodburning stove.

B. Identifying the Uses of Gerund Phrases
Underline the gerund phrases in these sentences. identify how each is used by writing **S** for subject, **DO** for direct object, **PN** for predicate nominative, **OP** for object of a preposition, or **A** for appositive.

1. Arguing with me takes much of my little brother's time. _____
2. The attorney helped his client by winning the jury's sympathy. _____
3. Roger loves reading about European cities. _____
4. Running around the field was part of the school fitness evaluation. _____
5. Mark uses his glasses only for reading. _____
6. Working long hours without a break can be counterproductive. _____
7. Alice began to devote time to her hobby, painting. _____
8. The first step for the candidate was winning in the primary. _____

Gerunds and Gerund Phrases

A. Identifying the Uses of Gerunds and Gerund Phrases

Underline each gerund or gerund phrase in these sentences. Identify how each is used by writing **S** for subject, **DO** for direct object, **PN** for predicate nominative, **OP** for object of a preposition, or **A** for appositive.

1. Playing paddle tennis is a new sport for me. _____

2. Played only as a doubles game, it requires practicing. _____

3. Playing with perforated wooden rackets is a strange sensation. _____

4. My tennis strategy, hitting the ball hard, did not work in this game. _____

5. After retrieving the soft rubber ball, I had to learn to lob it. _____

6. Now our winter enjoyment is playing paddle tennis. _____

7. Our only chore, shoveling the snow off the court, does not take long. _____

8. If the ball goes over the fence, our dog finds it by sniffing it out. _____

9. One problem in winter is getting enough exercise. _____

10. Athletes can stay in shape by playing paddle tennis. _____

B. Using Gerund Phrases

Combine the pairs of sentences below into one sentence with a gerund phrase.

1. His hobby became an obsession. His hobby is playing chess. _____

_____

2. Frank liked shop class. He liked to work with various tools there. _____

_____

3. He received recognition from his contemporaries. He became a more confident

writer. _____

_____

4. She wore green on St. Patrick's Day. It reminded her of her Irish heritage. _____

_____

5. Ricky hopes to achieve the dream of most baseball players. He hopes to be elected

to the National Baseball Hall of Fame. _____

_____

Clauses

A **clause** is a group of words that contains a subject and a verb. A clause that can stand alone as a sentence is an **independent,** or **main, clause.**

> After we arrived, *we met the mayor.* (The main clause is italicized.)

A clause that cannot stand alone as a sentence is a **subordinate,** or **dependent, clause.**

> Walloons are a Celtic people *who live in southern Belgium.* (The subordinate clause in italics cannot stand alone.)

Do not confuse a subordinate clause with a phrase. A phrase does not contain a subject and a verb, though it may contain a verbal—that is, an infinitive, a participle, or a gerund.

A. Identifying Clauses and Phrases

Identify each boldfaced group of words by writing **P** for a phrase and **C** for a clause.

1. Overshoes were once called arctics *since they were used in cold climates.* _____

2. The house fly has five eyes *located on the upper part of its head.* _____

3. *When the sun is close to the horizon,* it looks larger. _____

4. The king issued a proclamation *against shooting bears in the region.* _____

5. The growth of a tree splits the bark vertically, *producing ridges.* _____

6. *While red lights repel birds,* white lights attract them. _____

7. The poet Aeschylus was reportedly killed *by a tortoise falling on his head.* _____

8. A full moon appears larger *as it emerges from behind clouds.* _____

B. Identifying Independent and Subordinate Clauses

Identify each boldfaced group of words by writing **IC** for independent clause and **SC** for a subordinate clause.

1. When Peter changed his clothes for the party, *he forgot to comb his hair.* _____

2. Coney Island once had a hotel *that was built in the form of an elephant.* _____

3. Since the ancient Romans were not good mathematicians, *they contributed* little to the development of this science. _____

4. *Since Isaiah moved to New York six months ago,* he has had three jobs. _____

5. The surgeon's recommendation was controversial *because the operation had* never been tried before. _____

6. *After Anthony worked all summer as a waiter,* he bought a car. _____

7. *There were no newspapers in America* until one was published in Boston in 1690. _____

Clauses

A. Identifying Phrases and Clauses

Identify each boldfaced group of words. Write **P** for a phrase, **IC** for an independent clause, and **SC** for a subordinate clause.

1. *If you have solved that puzzle,* I'll give you a more difficult one. _____

2. Found only in the teeth, *enamel is the hardest substance in the body.* _____

3. Please tell me *what is in the box.* _____

4. We saw the superintendent *climbing the stairs.* _____

5. The person *who is climbing the hill* is my mother. _____

6. *After making several comparisons,* Greg was ready to buy a stereo. _____

7. This is the computer game *that I sent for.* _____

8. *Striding down the hall,* Mr. Sims looked neither right nor left. _____

9. *When I came home,* I found my brother had arrived there ahead of me. _____

10. Standing in the rain at the parade, *Fred got drenched.* _____

B. Using Clauses

Rewrite each sentence, adding a subordinate clause that begins with the word in parentheses.

Example   We thought that the man was joking. (until)
               We thought that the man was joking until we noticed the fire
               ourselves.

1. George Washington was commander-in-chief of the Continental Army. (before) _____

_____

2. We were just sitting down to dinner. (when) _____

_____

3. My mother does not approve of my watching TV. (unless) _____

_____

4. We would have won the game. (if) _____

_____

5. French is the language. (that) _____

_____

Adjective Clauses

An **adjective clause** is a subordinate clause that is used as an adjective to modify a noun or a pronoun. An adjective clause tells *what kind* or *which one*. It is usually placed immediately after the word it modifies. Most adjective clauses begin with a **relative pronoun:** *who, whom, whose, that, which.*

> The counselor told stories *that kept the campers awake all night.* (The adjective clause tells what kind of stories.

The **relative adverbs** *after, before, since, when, where,* and *why* may also introduce adjective clauses.

> We planned to visit Springfield, Massachusetts, *where basketball was invented.* (The adjective clause modifies *Springfield, Massachusetts.*)

An **essential adjective clause** is one that is needed to make the intended meaning of a sentence complete.

> We need a player *who can score.* (The adjective clause is essential to tell what kind of player is needed.)

A **nonessential adjective clause** is one that adds additional information to a sentence in which the meaning is already complete. Nonessential clauses are set off by commas.

> John Jacobs, *who is in our science class,* has the measles. (The adjective clause could be deleted and the sentence would still make sense.)

Identifying Adjective Clauses

Underline the adjective clause in each sentence. in the blank, write the word each adjective clause modifies.

1. Ed gave the package to his father, who will mail it tomorrow. _____

2. Lesotho is a country that is surrounded by another country. _____

3. Mountain gorillas, which are an endangered species, lives only in Africa. _____

4. The man whom you met is the theater manager. _____

5. I read "The Secret Sharer" by Joseph Conrad, who was born in Poland. _____

6. Something that always bothers me is a large crowd. _____

7. What was the date when Neil Armstrong stepped on the moon? _____

8. The poet T. S. Eliot, who was born in the United States, became a British subject. _____

9. The music that you heard was composed by our group. _____

10. The person whose name heads the list had to default. _____

11. Hawaii is an island where pineapples grow abundantly. _____

12. The llama, which is a member of the camel family, is found in South America. _____

Adjective Clauses

A. Identifying Essential and Nonessential Adjective Clauses

Underline the adjective clause in each sentence. In the blank, write **E** (for essential) or **NE** (for nonessential) to identify each adjective clause. Add necessary commas for nonessential clauses.

1. The Galápagos are known as the place where giant tortoises are found. _____

2. The legend about Captain Hook is one that has never been authenticated. _____

3. Beaver tail which I have never tried is regarded as a delicacy. _____

4. May gave the key to her mother who opened the door. _____

5. The winner of the essay contest that I entered will be announced today. _____

6: Cans, shoes, and clothing are among the things that goats will nibble. _____

7. The ship *Princess* which sailed around the island was built here. _____

8. The cross-country team is curious about the course that it will run. _____

9. Matt called the boys whom he had selected for the team. _____

10. Those friends usually meet a Hoffman's cafe where the food is cheap. _____

B. Using Adjective Clauses

Rewrite each of these sentences, adding an adjective clause to modify the boldfaced noun. Be sure to add necessary commas if the clause is nonessential.

> **Example**   Is this the *train?*
> **Is this the train that goes to Rochester?**

1. The *book* has finally been returned to the library. _____

_____

2. Leon's parents bought the *sweater.* _____

_____

3. Tom Selleck is an *actor.* _____

_____

4. This is the *season.* _____

_____

5. When did you open the *letter?* _____

_____

Adverb Clauses

An **adverb clause** is a subordinate clause that is used as an adverb to modify a verb, an adjective, or an adverb. An adverb clause tells *where, when, why, how,* or *to what extent.* It always begins with a **subordinating conjunction** such as *after, before, since, although, because, as, than, when, while, so that, until,* or *if.*

> The teacher mailed the letter *after she had sealed it.* (The adverb clause tells when the letter was mailed.)

A. Identifying Adverb Clauses

Underline the adverb clauses in the following sentences.

1. If the colonists hadn't protested, British taxes would have increased.

2. Because that clerk was so helpful, I praised her to the store manager.

3. Vince becomes nervous when he speaks in public.

4. Please visit us whenever you are in the Wilmington area.

5. According to legend, Nero fiddled while Rome burned.

6. Children should use car safety seats until they are four years old.

7. Although overcrowding is a problem in national parks, tourists continue to come.

8. After Bob arrived in Madrid, he began to study art.

9. This terrain will be useless unless it is irrigated.

10. As long as slavery continued, the southern economy prospered.

B. Identifying the Words That Adverb Clauses Modify

Underline the adverb clause in each of the following sentences. In the blank, write the word or words that each adverb clause modifies.

1. The movie was beginning as George bought our tickets. _____

2. When he was in his eighties, Dr. Seiler played in a string quartet. _____

3. Since he joined a health club, Will has gotten more exercise. _____

4. Whenever you make a promise, you must keep it! _____

5. Marlene can swim better than many professional swimmers can. _____

6. Although I'd not been in their house before, I felt at home right away. _____

7. Before the snow began, we stacked two cords of firewood. _____

8. You may have the job if you will work hard at it. _____

9. In a well-known Ronald Reagan movie, George Gipp ("the Gipper") was dying in a hospital while his coach sat by him. _____

10. When the Nineteenth Amendment to the United States Constitution was ratified in 1920, women finally received the right to vote. _____

Adverb Clauses

A. Identifying the Words That Adverb Clauses Modify

Underline the adverb clause in each of the following sentences. In the blank, write the word or words each adverb clause modifies.

Example   <u>When she is ready</u>, she will tell us.   **will tell**

1. Juan and Jorge returned before the period was over.   _____

2. He was late for work because he had missed the bus.   _____

3. Erica worked so that she could earn her college tuition.   _____

4. If Dr. Watson had not assisted him, Sherlock Holmes might not have solved some of his cases.   _____

5. Before you make a judgment, look into the matter carefully.   _____

6. She would not leave the piano until she had finished practicing.   _____

7. He will return after the ball game ends.   _____

8. She is faster than any other swimmer.   _____

9. Although I may be mistaken, I think that is already done.   _____

10. When acid rain affects a lake, plants and animals in the lake may die.   _____

B. Using Adverb Clauses

Compose sentences that use the following adverb clauses. If the clause is preceded by an ellipsis (three dots), put the adverb clause at the end of the sentence.

Example   . . . until you arrive.
                      We won't begin until you arrive.

1. Because the weather was bad, _____

_____

2. . . . because she was the fastest runner in the school. _____

_____

3. When the music began, _____

_____

4. If you get your driver's license, _____

_____

5. . . . while I am in the cafeteria. _____

_____

Noun Clauses

A **noun clause** is a subordinate clause that is used as a noun in a sentence. Noun clauses function as subjects, direct objects, indirect objects, predicate nominatives, and objects of prepositions. Noun clauses are introduced by pronouns such as *who, whom, which, what,* and *that;* and by subordinating conjunctions such as *how, that, when, where, whether,* and *why.*

> *Where she lives* is near the ocean. (subject)
> I believe *that her story is true.* (direct object)
> Give *whoever arrives* a copy of the report. (indirect object)
> An old saying is *that pride goeth before a fall.* (predicate nominative)
> She could see him from *where she stood.* (object of a preposition)

A. Identifying Noun Clauses

Underline the noun clause in each of these sentences.

1. No one knows who invented the wheel.

2. My favorite time of year is when the leaves change colors.

3. The store's delivery service will give priority to whoever calls first.

4. That the moon affects the tides is a scientific fact.

5. The glare of the sun was what affected the infielder's performance.

6. Did you understand what Darryl was saying?

7. Where the meeting will take place next has not been decided.

B. Identifying the Uses of Noun Clauses

Underline the noun clause in each sentence. In the blanks, identify the function of each noun clause: **S** for subject, **DO** for direct object, **IO** for indirect object, **PN** for predicate nominative, or **OP** for object of a preposition.

> **Example**   Heinrich Schliemann's belief was <u>that Troy actually existed</u>.
> **PN**

1. This guidebook is what you need for your backpacking tour of Europe. _____

2. They described the social system under which they live. _____

3. The classified advertisements will show where you can find a job. _____

4. Whoever wins the primary election will run in the general election this fall. _____

5. The dentist said that I had no cavities. _____

6. That Socrates believed in democracy is questionable. _____

7. There is no excuse for what happened today. _____

8. The committee will award whoever comes in first a special cup. _____

Noun Clauses

A. Identifying Noun Clauses

Underline the noun clauses in these sentences. In the blanks, identify the function of each noun clause: **S** for subject, **DO** for direct object, **IO** for indirect object, **OP** for object of a preposition, or **PN** for predicate nominative.

1. Did you know that Woody Allen's real name is Allen Konigsberg? _____

2. Whoever called didn't let the phone ring long enough. _____

3. They had no hint of what might happen. _____

4. The debate topic can be whatever you choose. _____

5. The response was what she expected. _____

6. I gave whoever asked the company's address. _____

7. Mr. Barnes swore that he would tell the truth. _____

8. What happened on June 8, 1990, will never be forgotten here. _____

9. No one knew where the equipment could be found. _____

10. You are always responsible for what you say. _____

B. Using Noun Clauses

Write sentences using the following noun clauses as indicated in parentheses.

> **Example**   who won the raffle (subject)
> **Who won the raffle is still not determined.**

1. why the experiment failed (direct object) _____

_____

2. whichever candidate gets the most votes (object of preposition) _____

_____

3. what every coach wants (predicate nominative) _____

_____

4. whoever comes to the door (indirect object) _____

_____

5. That you have seen the same things before (subject)_____

_____

The Structure of the Sentence

A **simple sentence** contains one independent clause and no subordinate clauses. A simple sentence may have any number of phrases.

> The tundra is a treeless plain of the arctic region.

A **compound sentence** has two or more independent clauses that are joined together. The clauses in a compound sentence may be joined (1) with a comma and a coordinating conjunction *(and, but, nor, or, for, yet);* (2) with a semicolon; or (3) with a semicolon and a conjunctive adverb (such as *however* or *therefore*).

> Most tundras are lowlands, but some have mountains.
> The subsoil is permanently frozen; it is called permafrost.
> Winters are frigid; however, many animals live on the tundra.

A **complex sentence** consists of one main clause and one or more subordinate clauses. The subordinate clause is used as a noun or as a modifier.

> Lichens and moss, which grow in the tundra, survive in surface soil.

A **compound-complex sentence** has two or more independent clauses and one or more subordinate clauses.

> Greenland has a permafrost that is at least 2,000 feet deep, and in other places the frozen subsoil may be even deeper.

Identifying the Structure of the Sentence

Underline all independent clauses, and place parentheses around all subordinate clauses in these sentences. In the blank, identify the structure of the sentence by writing **S** (simple), **C** (compound), **CX** (complex), or **CC** (compound-complex).

> **Example**   T. S. Eliot is a well-known poet (who also wrote plays).   **CX**

1. When the rain began, we were playing soccer. _____

2. Beth enjoys all seasons, but she likes fall best. _____

3. Although Franklin Delano Roosevelt's health was failing, he ran for president

   a fourth time in 1944, and he won. _____

4. My sister enjoys chemistry, history, and English. _____

5. If you want your car cleaned, let George wash it. _____

6. When I am tired, I am not good company for friends who want a jokester. _____

7. Mickey worked all morning, and then, when he was finished, he relaxed. _____

8. How many states can you see from the top of Lookout Mountain? _____

9. Midori is a violin prodigy who is becoming internationally famous. _____

10. Australia, which is the continent "down under," was first settled by the

    ancestors of the Aborigines; European settlers arrived there in 1788. _____

The Structure of the Sentence

A. Identifying the Structure of the Sentence

Identify the structure of each of these sentences. In the blank, write **S** for simple, **C** for compound, **CX** for complex, or **CC** for compound-complex.

1. After defeating Germany in World War II, the Allies divided Germany and its capital city, Berlin, into four sectors—a British sector, a French sector, an American sector, and a Russian sector. _____

2. The British, French, and American sectors became the Federal Republic of Germany. _____

3. The Russian sector became the German Democratic Republic, or East Germany, and Berlin is in that sector. _____

4. The East Germans tried to make Berlin their capital, but ultimately they could only have East Berlin because the Americans, French, and British controlled West Berlin. _____

5. East Germans who tried to cross the border to West Germany were prevented from doing so by East German border guards, mines, and barbed wire. _____

6. Many East Germans escaped to the West by taking the subway from East Berlin to West Berlin; from West Berlin they could reach other western cities. _____

7. Because so many people escaped, East Germany did not have enough workers, and a wall was erected between East Berlin and West Berlin. _____

8. In 1989 the Berlin Wall came down, and the two Germanys were united the following year. _____

B. Building Sentences

Build sentences by adding words, phrases, and clauses to the simple sentence below. Keep the structures from the preceding sentences in each new sentence.

That girl sings.

1. Add an adjective and an adverb to the sentence. _____

_____

2. Now add a prepositional phrase. _____

_____

3. Add another independent clause. _____

_____

4. Add a subordinate clause. _____

_____

Sentence Fragments

A **sentence fragment** is a group of words that is only part of a sentence. A sentence must have at least one subject and one verb. It must also express a complete thought.

> The merchants of the city. (Did what? The verb is missing.)

Many sentence fragments occur because the writer inserts end punctuation and a capital letter too soon. To complete such fragments you must sometimes add or delete words.

Fragment   *While she was reading.* She fell asleep.
Sentence   While she was reading, she fell asleep.

A. Correcting Fragments Caused by Incomplete Thoughts
Add words to change the sentence fragments into sentences.

1. While waiting for computer time. _____

_____

2. Intelligence tests in education. _____

_____

3. Before the broadcast had even started. _____

_____

4. A successful fly fisherman and a student of entomology. _____

_____

5. Working to save the tropical rain forests. _____

_____

B. Correcting Fragments Caused by Incorrect Punctuation
Make any changes necessary to combine each pair of fragments into a sentence.

1. The invention of electricity. Made gas lights obsolete. _____

_____

2. Because television requires no feedback. Viewers become passive. _____

_____

3. In 1869 celluloid, the first synthetic plastic. Was invented. _____

_____

4. Crossing the street with two bags of groceries. Stumbled and fell. _____

_____

5. Although Gina speaks Italian fluently. Has never visited Italy. _____

_____

Sentence Fragments

A. Recognizing and Correcting Fragments

Find the sentence fragments in the following hastily written paragraph on snakes. Then, on the lines below, combine the fragments or add words to make complete sentences. If a numbered group of words is already a sentence, write the number and the word **sentence** on the line.

(1) May not like snakes but can marvel at their success as predators. (2) No limbs for grabbing and holding prey. (3) Use effectively the tools they do have. (4) Long, coiling bodies. (5) Allow them to reach prey in seemingly unreachable places. (6) Their flexible jaws allow them to eat things that appear much too big. (7) Their venom. (8) Works in ways appropriate to particular snakes' habitats and typical prey. (9) As part of nature's food chain. (10) Often themselves become the prey of other predators.

_____

_____

_____

_____

_____

_____

_____

B. Correcting Fragments Within a Paragraph

Rewrite each of the numbered pairs of word groups to eliminate the fragment. Change punctuation and capitalization, and delete words as necessary.

(1) Penguins squeal and squawk loudly. As a means of greeting one another. (2) Wings, which do not permit flight. Make them excellent swimmers. (3) Penguins waddle over the snow. But dive and leap effortlessly in the water. (4) They spend most of their time in the ocean. Heading for land mainly to lay their eggs and raise their young. (5) The chicks, or young penguins. They need care in their first six months of life.

1. _____

2. _____

3. _____

4. _____

   _____

5. _____

Phrases as Fragments

A phrase does not contain both a subject and a verb. Thus a phrase cannot be a sentence; it can only be a fragment. Phrases such as those shown below should not be confused with sentences.

Prepositional Phrase	At the showroom
Complete Sentence	New cars are arriving at the showroom.
Participial Phrase	Having read the newspaper.
Complete Sentence	Having read the newspaper, Joshua decided to shoot some baskets.
Gerund Phrase	Living in New York City.
Complete Sentence	Living in New York City is stimulating.
Infinitive Phrase	To attend the concert.
Complete Sentence	Maura plans to attend the concert.
Appositive Phrase	An unusual model.
Complete Sentence	Her new calculator, an unusual model, is the size of a credit card.

Correcting Fragments

Correct each of the following sentence fragments by writing a complete sentence. Use one of the types of corrections shown above.

1. On the flight to Argentina. _____

_____

2. To run the mile in less than four minutes. _____

_____

3. In the room at the back of the house. _____

_____

4. A book about growing plants indoors. _____

_____

5. Focusing the picture. _____

_____

6. To present our case before the Governor. _____

_____

7. Using geometric shapes. _____

_____

8. Speeding on the highway. _____

_____

Phrases as Fragments

A. Correcting Fragments
Add the words necessary to change each fragment into a complete sentence.

1. Seeing Earth from outer space. _____

   _____

2. In the cargo bay. _____

   _____

3. A veteran of three space flights. _____

   _____

4. Performing scientific experiments for NASA. _____

   _____

5. To stay in good physical condition. _____

   _____

B. Correcting Fragments Within a Paragraph
Expand the following notes into a paragraph. Rewrite the fragments in each numbered item, joining word groups or adding words as necessary to make complete sentences.

> **(1)** Living alone is not as safe for elephants. Living safer in a herd. **(2)** To guard their young from an approaching danger. Elephants huddling together in a circle. **(3)** In answer to a threat. An enormous female breaking away from the circle and charging. **(4)** Defending the group. By frightening the enemy. **(5)** This behavior is typical. For wild elephants.

1. _____

   _____

2. _____

   _____

3. _____

   _____

4. _____

5. _____

Clauses as Fragments

Although a subordinate clause has both a subject and a verb, it does not express a complete thought and is therefore a fragment. Combine a subordinate clause with an independent clause to correct this kind of fragment.

Fragment While we were waiting
Revision While we were waiting, we read yesterday's newspaper.

Another way to correct a fragment like this is to rewrite the clause as a sentence.

Fragment Glacier National Park, which is in northwestern Montana
Revision Glacier National Park is in northwestern Montana.

A. Identifying Sentence Fragments
Read each group of words below. If the group is a sentence, write **S** on the line. If the group is a fragment, write **F** on the line.

1. Since a warranty guarantees a product for a certain length of time.   _____

2. Unless you have a written warranty for expensive and inexpensive items.   _____

3. If a product is delivered to you and it is broken.   _____

4. Because most companies want satisfaction for all their customers.   _____

5. We passed new legislation, which gives consumers more protection.   _____

B. Changing Fragments into Sentences
Rewrite each subordinate clause to form a complete sentence. Combine the clause with an independent clause or rewrite it as a sentence.

1. Kamel, who is in my geometry class.

_____

2. Because I have been walking for three hours.

_____

3. My father's new car, which is parked in the driveway.

_____

4. Since Sylvia started her new job.

_____

5. Before we move to the South.

_____

6. Lassen Peak, which is a dormant volcano.

_____

Clauses as Fragments

A. Changing Fragments into Sentences

Rewrite each subordinate clause to form a complete sentence, combining it with an independent clause or adding words as necessary.

1. Although she is new in school. Julie was elected class president.

   _____

2. After our English class read the folktale.

   _____

3. The audience applauded. When the astronaut finished her address.

   _____

4. Andrew, who played the lead in the class play.

   _____

5. While the country waited.

   _____

Correcting Fragments Within a Paragraph

Rewrite the numbered items to eliminate the sentence fragments.

> **(1)** Bears are very adaptable creatures. Which are found on nearly every continent. **(2)** Bears can run at a speed of twenty-five miles per hour. Although they are normally slow-paced. **(3)** The area in which they live. It includes mountains, forests, and tundra. **(4)** Different kinds of bears thrive in different settings. Because these animals eat a variety of different foods. **(5)** Although we often think of bears roaming about on land. Excellent climbers and swimmers.

1. _____

2. _____

   _____

3. _____

   _____

4. _____

   _____

5. _____

   _____

Run-on Sentences

A **run-on sentence** is two or more sentences written incorrectly as one.
Sometimes the best way to correct a run-on is to break it into separate sentences.

Run-on	The snow is melting rapidly low areas will flood tonight.
Revision	**The snow is melting rapidly. Low areas will flood tonight.**

When the ideas are closely related, it is better to join them into a single sentence.
You can join them with a comma and a coordinating conjunction.

Run-on	He was delayed on the train, he still arrived on time.
Revision	**He was delayed on the train, but he still arrived on time.**

You can join the sentences with a semicolon.

Run-on	Night was falling the sun was setting.
Revision	**Night was falling; the sun was setting.**

You can join the sentences with a semicolon and a conjunctive adverb.

Run-on	A diamond won't dissolve in acid, intense heat can destroy it.
Revision	**A diamond won't dissolve in acid; however, intense heat** can destroy it.

Revising Run-on Sentences

Revise the run-on sentences below, using the method given in parentheses.

1. In 1818, when she was twenty-one, Mary Shelley wrote *Frankenstein*, a "masterpiece of horror," the book has been popular ever since. (Break into two.)

   _____

   _____

2. The tale started as a parlor game, a group of friends sat by the fire telling ghost stories. (Join with a semicolon.)

   _____

3. That night Mary had a vivid dream she imagined how a monster might be created by bringing a corpse back to life. (Break into two.)

   _____

   _____

4. Many films center on Frankenstein's monster few of them deal with the book's serious themes. (Join with a semicolon and a conjunctive adverb.)

   _____

5. The original story is more than a simple horror tale, it deals with the darker side of scientific discovery. (Join with a semicolon.)

   _____

   _____

Run-on Sentences

A. Revising Run-on Sentences

Revise the run-on sentences below, using punctuation marks, coordinating conjunctions, and conjunctive adverbs where needed.

1. In 1849, Walter Hunt designed a pin with a clasp to enclose it, he might not have created the "safe" pin if he hadn't owed money.

   _____

   _____

2. His creditor offered to cancel Hunt's fifteen-dollar debt, in fact, the creditor offered four hundred dollars for the rights to any useful device Hunt could create from an old piece of wire.

   _____

   _____

3. Hunt twisted the wire for three hours he devised the modern safety pin.

   _____

4. Hunt collected the promised four hundred dollars, his creditor made a fortune.

   _____

B. Correcting Run-on Sentences

Revise each run-on sentence. Write the corrected sentences on the lines below.

   (1) About 1440, Johannes Gutenberg perfected the process of printing with movable type blocks his system used separate pieces of raised metal type. (2) Movable type was not new, it had been tried earlier in China and Korea. (3) Movable type was impractical in those countries because of the complexity of the languages, Gutenberg worked with the much simpler Roman alphabet. (4) In earlier times, books had been copied by hand, with Gutenberg's invention, multiple copies could be made quickly and easily.

1. _____

   _____

2. _____

3. _____

   _____

4. _____

   _____

Directions One or more of the underlined sections in the following sentences may contain errors of grammar, usage, punctuation, spelling, or capitalization. Write the letter of each incorrect section; then rewrite the item correctly. If there is no error in an item, write *E.* Write your answers on your own paper or on an answer sheet, as your teacher directs.

Example   Did the ancient <u>egyptian</u> <u>navy</u> include <u>long ships</u> powered by
                              A   **B**   **C**

            oarsmen and <u>sails.</u> <u>No error</u>
                     D   **E**

Answer   A—Egyptian   D—sails?

1. The <u>Mexican</u> revolutionary <u>Pancho Villa</u> made El Paso his <u>headquarters. During</u>
    A   **B**   **C**

    the early <u>1900's.</u> <u>No error</u>
             D   **E**

2. <u>Deep beneath the Texas sand</u> <u>is</u> huge deposits of <u>natural gas</u> the <u>cleanest</u> fossil
            A   **B**   **C**   **D**

    fuel. <u>No error</u>
        E

3. <u>Nebraska</u> has a unique form of <u>government. its</u> <u>state legislature</u> <u>at Lincoln</u> has
    A   **B**   **C**   **D**

    only one house. <u>No error</u>
                   E

4. Peasants <u>in the Middle Ages</u> legally belonged to the lord <u>on whose</u> land <u>they lived;</u>
            A   **B**   **C**

    <u>however,</u> many were able to escape to freedom in nearby towns. <u>No error</u>
    D   **E**

5. The music for our national anthem <u>was composed</u> by an <u>Englishman</u> John
                                  A   **B**

    Stafford Smith, in the late <u>1700's the lyrics</u> <u>were written</u> in 1814 by Francis Scott
                              C   **D**

    Key. <u>No error</u>
         E

6. <u>That's extraordinary.</u> An <u>elephant's</u> <u>skin</u> which is about 1.5 inches <u>thick,</u> weighs
    A   **B**   **C**   **D**

    almost a ton. <u>No error</u>
                E

7. The <u>British</u> archaeologist <u>Howard Carter</u> created worldwide <u>intrest</u> in
       A   B   C

   <u>archaeology: when</u> he found King Tutankhamen's tomb in Egypt. <u>No error</u>
         D   E

8. After the date of <u>New Years Day</u> was changed to <u>January 1 people</u> who continued
                    A   B   C

   to celebrate the old date, <u>April 1,</u> came to be known as "April fools." <u>No error</u>
                                  D   E

9. American <u>artists</u> of the movement known as the <u>ashcan school</u> revolted against
            A   B

   sentimental subject <u>matter they</u> preferred to paint slums, <u>factories,</u> and other
                          C   D

   down-to-earth scenes. <u>No error</u>
                       E

10. High above nearby buildings <u>soar</u> the 1,454-foot <u>Sears Tower. The</u> <u>world's</u> <u>tallest</u>
                              A   B   C   D

   skyscraper. <u>No error</u>
               E

11. <u>Ellis Island</u> is the historic spot in New York <u>harbor. Where</u> <u>thousand's</u> of
      A   B   C

   <u>immigrants entered</u> the United States. <u>No error</u>
         D   E

12. <u>"The Raven,"</u> a <u>poem which</u> was <u>written</u> by Edgar Allan <u>Poe, is</u> often read by high
      A   B   C   D

   school students. <u>No error</u>
                   E

13. Wasn't the <u>exhibit</u> <u>that we saw</u> at the science museum <u>the most</u> spectacular one
                A   B   C

   you <u>have ever seen?</u> <u>No error</u>
       D   E

14. Martha <u>Graham's father</u> <u>disapproved</u> of her interest in <u>dance but</u> Graham
             A   B   C

   <u>eventually became</u> one of the pioneering leaders of modern dance. <u>No error</u>
      D   E

15. What an <u>enormous</u> impact the <u>cartoonist Walt</u> <u>Disney had</u> on the imaginations of
           A   B   C

   children all over the <u>world?</u> <u>No error</u>
                   D   E

Directions Some part or all of each sentence is underlined. Choose the best way to rewrite the underlined section. If the underlined section needs no change, choose answer **A.** Write your answers on your own paper or on an answer sheet, as your teacher directs.

Example   <u>Around A.D. 100 the Chinese invented paper</u> Arabs learned the process in the eighth century.
A. Around A.D. 100 the Chinese invented paper
B. Around A.D. 100 the Chinese invented paper?
C. Around A.D. 100 the Chinese invented paper.
D. Around A.D. 100 the Chinese invented paper:

Answer   C

16. <u>Accused of murder, the jury found Lizzie Borden not guilty.</u>
A. Accused of murder, the jury found Lizzie Borden not guilty.
B. The jury, accused of murder, found Lizzie Borden not guilty.
C. The jury found Lizzie Borden not guilty accused of murder.
D. The jury found Lizzie Borden, accused of murder, not guilty.

17. <u>Brambles, prickly shrubs that belong to the rose family.</u>
A. Brambles, prickly shrubs that belong to the rose family.
B. Brambles are prickly shrubs that belong to the rose family.
C. Brambles, that belong to the rose family, are prickly shrubs.
D. Brambles belong to the rose family, they are prickly shrubs.

18. <u>Working overtime for six weeks, the stage sets were finished in time.</u>
A. Working overtime for six weeks, the stage sets were finished in time.
B. The stage sets were finished in time, working overtime for six weeks.
C. Working overtime for six weeks, the stage sets were finished in time by the crew.
D. Working overtime for six weeks, the crew finished the stage sets in time.

19. <u>Most people in Belgium speak Dutch; however, French in this bilingual country is the second official language</u>.
A. Most people in Belgium speak Dutch; however, French in this bilingual country is the second official language.
B. Most people in Belgium speak Dutch in this bilingual country; however, French is the second official language.
C. Most people in Belgium speak Dutch; however, French is the second official language in this bilingual country.
D. Most people in Belgium speak Dutch, however, French is the second official language in this bilingual country.

20. <u>Brazil's coastal plain, which lies along the Atlantic and has large areas of fertile soil.</u>
A. Brazil's coastal plain, which lies along the Atlantic and has large areas of fertile soil.
B. Brazil's coastal plain, that lies along the Atlantic, has large areas of fertile soil.
C. Brazil's coastal plain, which lies along the Atlantic, has large areas of fertile soil.
D. Brazil's coastal plain, which lies along the Atlantic, and has large areas of fertile soil.

The Principal Parts of Verbs (I)

The principal parts of the verb are the **present infinitive** (usually called the **present**), the **present participle**, the **past**, and the **past participle**. The present participle is the *-ing* form of the verb. The past tense form is used alone; the past participle is used with forms of *have*. The past and the past participle may be formed in several ways.

A **regular verb** forms its past and past participle by adding *-d* or *-ed* to the present form of the verb: *walk, walked, (have) walked*. Most verbs in English are regular.

An **irregular verb** does not form its past and past participle by adding *-d* or *-ed* to the present form of the verb. About sixty commonly used verbs are irregular.

Some irregular verbs have the same form for the present, the past, and the past participle.

Present	Present Participle	Past	Past Participle
burst	(is) bursting	burst	(have) burst
cost	(is) costing	cost	(have) cost
hit	(is) hitting	hit	(have) hit
shut	(is) shutting	shut	(have) shut

Other irregular verbs have the same form for both the past and the past participle.

Present	Present Participle	Past	Past Participle
bring	(is) bringing	brought	(have) brought
fling	(is) flinging	flung	(have) flung
get	(is) getting	got	(have) got, gotten
lend	(is) lending	lent	(have) lent
lead	(is) leading	led	(have) led

Using Verbs Correctly

Underline the correct verb in each of the following sentences.

1. The Spanish (brang, brought) the first horses to America.

2. The new bridge has (cost, costed) the city a great deal of money.

3. Emilio (swang, swung) the bat so hard that he lost his balance.

4. The principal informed us that the water pipes had (burst, bursted).

5. I have (hitted, hit) more home runs this year than I ever did before.

6. Karen (lended, lent) Ken a book three weeks ago, and he hasn't returned it yet.

7. Before she left, Marta (shut, shutted) the supply cabinet doors tightly.

8. The zoo keeper has (flinged, flung) a net over the rampaging tiger.

9. Mr. and Mrs. Stark have (leaded, led) the campaign to enact a leash law.

10. Teresa has (sang, sung) in the school chorus for one year so far.

11. The spectators' remarks (stung, stinged) the players as they filed defeated from the arena.

12. Mr. Frost had (teached, taught) English to sophomores for eleven years.

13. Margaret (got, getted) some commemorative stamps at the post office.

14. The prosecutor has (ask, asked) the judge to dismiss the case entirely.

15. Have the speakers (brang, brought) along any audiovisuals?

The Principal Parts of Verbs (I)

A. Using Verbs Correctly

In the following sentences, underline the verb forms used incorrectly and write the correct forms in the blanks. If a sentence has no verb errors, write **Correct** in the blank.

1. Jonathan bursted into the room after realizing that the uncaged canary and the cat were in there together. _____

2. Rebecca led the team to a glorious victory. _____

3. The historical society has fighted the building's demolition. _____

4. Working hard to promote literacy, volunteers have teached many basic skills. _____

5. Your double-scoop ice cream cone cost too much! _____

6. While the host was greeting newcomers, one of the guests setted the table. _____

7. After being stinged by the wasp, the howling child ran to his older sister. _____

8. As soon as I arrived home, I put my books aside. It was Friday! _____

9. Judy and Peter brang pickles and olives to the all-school picnic. _____

10. Tim suddenly remembered that he forgetted to pack his boots. _____

11. We hauled two trash bags to the dumpster and flinged them inside. _____

12. Mrs. Weir lended her son the car with the understanding that he would be home by eleven. _____

13. Because of the raging storm, many people have fleed to the countryside. _____

14. Our best batter hit four home runs in the last game. _____

15. Mia caught, cleaned, grilled, and eaten a huge bluefish. _____

B. Using the Past and Past Participle

Write sentences using each of the following verbs in the form indicated in parentheses.

> **Example**   bring (past participle)
> **I have brought** enough dessert for everybody.

1. give (past)_____

2. talk (past) _____

3. get (past participle)_____

4. fight (past) _____

5. put (past participle)_____

The Principal Parts of Verbs (II)

Some irregular verbs add -n or -en to the past form to make the past participle.

Present	Present Participle	Past	Past Participle
bear	(is) bearing	bore	(have) borne
bite	(is) biting	bit	(have) bitten
choose	(is) choosing	chose	(have) chosen
freeze	(is) freezing	froze	(have) froze
wear	(is) wearing	wore	(have) worn

Other irregular verbs change the middle vowel from *i* in the present, to *a* in the past, and to *u* in the past participle.

Present	Present Participle	Past	Past Participle
begin	(is) beginning	began	(have) begun
drink	(is) drinking	drank	(have) drunk
sing	(is) singing	sang	(have) sung
spring	(is) springing	sprang, sprung	(have) sprung
swim	(is) swimming	swam	(have) swum

Using the Past and the Past Participle

In each blank, write the past or the past participle of the verb in parentheses as appropriate.

1. President Lincoln (bear) his troubles bravely.   _____

2. Mario has (sing) in several high school musicals.   _____

3. Anna hasn't (begin) to think about her choice of colleges yet.   _____

4. As John Smith was about to die, Pocahontas (spring) to his rescue.   _____

5. Paul (bite) into the granola bar greedily.   _____

6. I have already (freeze) the blueberries we picked yesterday.   _____

7. Traditionally, the villagers have (wear) elaborate costumes.   _____

8. Which movie had you (choose) to win the Academy Award?   _____

9. Juliet (drink) the potion and went into a deep sleep.   _____

10. The trapdoor (spring) open and the magician disappeared.   _____

11. I (wear) braces for three years.   _____

12. Henry Luce (begin) publishing *Time* magazine in 1923.   _____

13. Rene has (swim) in every competition this year.   _____

14. Americans have (drink) carbonated beverages since 1807.   _____

15. Many celebrities (sing) at the benefit concert.   _____

A. Using the Past and Past Participle

In the following sentences, change the verb in parentheses to the past or the past participle as appropriate and write it in the blank.

1. It was our group's turn to choose the afternoon activity. We (choose) swimming. _____

2. It was so hot that day that we all must have (drink) a gallon of water. _____

3. When we heard the whistle, we (spring) to our feet. _____

4. No one (speak) a word; we all ran for the pool. _____

5. Yolanda and I had a race to the pool; she had (beat) me before. _____

6. When we reached the pool, a bell (ring); we would have one hour to swim. _____

7. Some of the girls (wear) bathing caps in the pool. _____

8. I thought Yolanda had (steal) my towel, but I found it under a bench. _____

9. I (break) a camp record for swimming laps. _____

10. I even (beat) Yolanda back to the bunk. _____

B. Using Verbs Correctly

Underline the verbs used incorrectly in the paragraph below. Then write the correct form of the verb in the space above. The first one has been done for you.

        began
(1) The day begun in an interesting way—in the morning we were told that the camp was celebrating its fifth anniversary. (2) The camp director brought cider, and we drunk it all through the celebration. (3) That night we roasted hot dogs and singed songs around the campfire. (4) Unfortunately, someone had forgot to cover the mustard; when the new counselor picked up the jar, she was stung by a bee. (5) Giving a cry, she springed to her feet. (6) Once everyone had calmed down, the head counselor speaked to the group. (7) She talked about being a new counselor five years before; she remembered how the day had began. (8) Everyone laughed when she told how she had been bit by a bug on her first day! (9) The new counselor then speaked; she said that she couldn't wait for *her* fifth-year anniversary. (10) Then she, too, could laugh about how she had been "broked in" to camp life.

The Principal Parts of Verbs (III)

Another group of irregular verbs forms the past participle from the present. Some of the past participles are the same as the present form, while others add *-n* or *-en* to the present form. (*Go* and *do* add *-ne*.)

Present	Present Participle	Past	Past Participle
come	(is) coming	came	(have) come
do	(is) doing	did	(have) done
draw	(is) drawing	drew	(have) drawn
fall	(is) falling	fell	(have) fallen
go	(is) going	went	(have) gone
grow	(is) growing	grew	(have) grown
know	(is) knowing	knew	(have) known
run	(is) running	ran	(have) run
see	(is) seeing	saw	(have) seen
shake	(is) shaking	shook	(have) shaken
take	(is) taking	took	(have) taken
throw	(is) throwing	threw	(have) thrown
write	(is) writing	wrote	(have) written

Using the Past and the Past Participle

In each blank, write the past or the past participle of the verb in parentheses.

1. Sherlock Holmes (draw) his conclusions from careful observation. _____

2. That senatorial candidate has simply (run) out of energy. _____

3. Have you (take) your driver's license test yet? _____

4. The city health inspector (come) to investigate complaints about the restaurant. _____

5. Be prepared to answer questions about work you have (do) in the past. _____

6. *The Pearl* was one of the best novels John Steinbeck ever (write). _____

7. I have never (know) a more patient person than Michelle. _____

8. Icarus (fall) to earth when the sun melted the wax on his wings. _____

9. The oak tree in our backyard has (grow) to an enormous height. _____

10. By the time the police arrived, the burglar had (go). _____

11. Paula had never (see) such dramatic flamenco dancing before. _____

12. William Slater has (write) many science-fiction novels. _____

13. Lindsay has (go) to the Middle East on an archaeological expedition. _____

14. If you hadn't (shake) the chemicals, the test tube wouldn't have exploded. _____

15. Did they catch the youngsters who (throw) the snowballs at the school bus?

The Principal Parts of Verbs (III)

A. Using the Past and the Past Participle
In the blank, write the past or the past participle of the verb in parentheses.

1. On our trip to Arizona, we (see) a number of spectacular sights. _____

2. I (know) when we reached Tucson that I had found my favorite place. _____

3. Tucson, Arizona's largest city, (become) part of the United States in 1853. _____

4. Many of Tucson's current residents first (come) to the area during World War II. _____

5. Since the mid-1960's, Tucson's population has (grow) very rapidly. _____

6. After I had (take) one long look at Mount Lemon amidst the beauty of the desert, I knew that this was a place I could live forever. _____

7. When we visited Saguaro National Monument, I wondered how all of the cactus had (grow) into so many sizes and shapes. _____

8. As we (ride) through the acres and acres of cactus, I was overwhelmed by the beauty of the desert. _____

B. Using Verbs Correctly
Underline the verbs used incorrectly in the paragraph below. Then write the correct form of the verb in the space above.

(1) We could see many varieties of cactuses as we rided through the deserts of Tucson. (2) I was amazed to see that all of these different kinds of cactuses—crown of thorns, rosette succulents, prickly pear, and seguro—growed side by side. (3) On our second day in Tucson, we gone to visit the Arizona-Sonora Desert Museum. (4) We had already ate lunch, so we had a full afternoon to spend at the museum. (5) Some of the best exhibits we seen were dioramas of Arizona wildlife. (6) It seemed I had took several hours to study how real the animals and plants looked in these displays. (7) In one diorama, I seen coyotes howling at a full moon. (8) In another, roadrunners runned in carefree style across the fields. (9) The day ended too quickly; however, I write postcards to all of my friends while the sights of the Desert Museum were still fresh in my mind. (10) We wished that we had went to the Kitt Peak National Observatory. (11) Unfortunately, we run out of time. (12) If we had knew how wonderful Tucson was, we would have planned to stay much longer.

Verb Tenses

Verbs change form to show the time of the action they express. These changes in form are called **tenses.** Every verb has six tenses.

present: I work.   **present perfect:** I have worked.
past: I worked.   **past perfect:** I had worked.
future: I will (shall) work.   **future perfect:** I will (shall) have worked.

A. Identifying Verb Tenses

Underline the verb in each sentence and write its tense in the blank.

1. I will support your candidacy for class president. _____

2. By Friday we will have sold all of the raffle tickets. _____

3. Their temperatures usually rise at night. _____

4. Lloyd left his bicycle at school over the weekend. _____

5. My sisters have mailed me five letters from college. _____

6. Archie had visited his friend during spring vacation. _____

7. I will have left by three o'clock. _____

8. We shall interview the five members of the crew. _____

9. The candidates have campaigned steadily for eighteen months. _____

10. Amy bought that funky hat at a flea market last Saturday. _____

B. Using Verb Tenses

On the line, write the verb in parentheses in the tense indicated.

1. Once the blockers (past perfect of *create*) a hole, Dan plunged through it. _____

2. Today (present of *promise*) to be a great day for fishing. _____

3. The press (past of *applaud*) respectfully as the Mayor entered the room. _____

4. "Tomorrow we (future of *experiment*) with sulfuric acid," said Ms. Ames. _____

5. We (present perfect of *grow*) tomatoes in this plot for the last ten years. _____

6. At this rate, Al (future perfect of *break*) two track records by the race's end. _____

7. "That rookie (future of *swing*) at anything," muttered the coach. _____

8. Before she ran for mayor, Ms. Jordan (past perfect of *garner*) much support. _____

9. By the end of December, she (future perfect of *save*) $4,000. _____

10. We (past perfect of *visit*) all of the Virginia battlefields by the end of the summer. _____

Verb Tenses

A. Identifying and Using Verb Tenses

Underline the verb in each sentence and write the tense above it. Then, on the line, write the verb in the tense indicated in parentheses.

                past
Example   Mia *wrote* a ballad. (present perfect) **has written**

1. The polyorchis jellyfish looked like an electric light bulb. (present) _____

2. By today the climbers will reach the summit. (future perfect) _____

3. New Zealand is the leading producer of kiwi fruit. (present perfect) _____

4. Jake played lacrosse for two years. (past perfect) _____

5. My great-grandmother turns one hundred years old this May. (future) _____

6. In 1971 Billie Jean King had won nineteen tennis tournaments. (past) _____

7. The famous pirate William Kidd was once an honest sea captain. (past perfect) _____

8. Rena's family moved twice in the last three years. (present perfect) _____

B. Using Verb Tenses

On the line, write the verb in parentheses in the tense indicated.

1. James Joyce was born in Ireland, but he (past of *live*) outside of the country for

   most of his adult life. _____

2. In Joyce's autobiographical novel, *A Portrait of the Artist as a Young Man,* the

   protagonist (present of *leave*) Ireland and becomes a writer. _____

3. Joyce's *Finnegan's Wake* (present perfect of *become*) a vehicle through which

   readers can study the author's "stream of consciousness" technique. _____

4. In writing *Ulysses,* which was published in 1922, Joyce (past perfect of *use*)

   Homer's *Odyssey* as a structural aid. _____

5. *Ulysses* (past of *lift*) Joyce out of a life of poverty and obscurity. _____

6. Joyce's work (present perfect of *change*) the shape of modern fiction. _____

7. By high school's end, most students (future perfect of *read*) some work by Joyce. _____

8. Generations of students (future of *continue*) to enjoy Joyce's masterpieces. _____

Progressive and Emphatic Verb Forms

The **progressive forms** of a verb are used to show ongoing action. Progressive forms are made by using forms of *be* with the present participle.

present progressive	She is singing.
past progressive	She was singing.
future progressive	She will be singing.
present perfect progressive	She has been singing.
past perfect progressive	She had been singing.
future perfect progressive	She will have been singing.

The **emphatic forms** are used to give special emphasis to the verb. Emphatic forms are made by using forms of *do* with the present form of the main verb.

present emphatic	I really do like the dessert.
past emphatic	He did arrive on time.

Identifying Progressive and Emphatic Forms of Verbs

Underline the verb in each of the following sentences. Then, in the blank, identify the progressive or emphatic form of each verb.

Example   Aspirin <u>does prevent</u> pain. **present emphatic**

They <u>were</u> still <u>trying</u> to water-ski. **past progressive**

1. Lorene has been experimenting with the new equipment in the laboratory. _____

2. Rosemary will be demonstrating her work at the craft show. _____

3. I did follow all of the instructions on the package! _____

4. Richard did hear you. _____

5. The choir is singing at the folk festival in May. _____

6. The Mayor does understand the need for better recreational facilities. _____

7. The three girls were deciding on a route for their bike trip. _____

8. It will be snowing by this time tomorrow afternoon. _____

9. My friends and I really do enjoy skiing. _____

10. The runners will be finishing the cross-country course. _____

11. Has Mindy been doing her homework lately? _____

12. The twins really did eat four ice cream cones. _____

13. They will have been living in Ashland for twenty years this June. _____

14. My sister had been taking tennis lessons before her accident. _____

15. Is she following the Mariners this year? _____

Progressive and Emphatic Verb Forms

Using Progressive and Emphatic Forms

On the line, write the verb in parentheses in the form indicated.

1. Cheryl and I (past progressive of *plan*) to ask the teacher about the assignment.

_____

2. Pauline (future progressive of *travel*) to Montana with her family this summer.

_____

3. Lester (past emphatic of *make*) the varsity team last year.

_____

4. In Japan, people (present perfect progressive of *eat*) tofu for centuries.

_____

5. Alpha Centauri (present emphatic of *shine*) more brightly than many other stars.

_____

6. Rosa (future perfect progressive of *compete*) in road races for six years this May.

_____

7. A secret British computer (past perfect progressive of *break*) Nazi codes for two years when the first U.S. electronic computer went into operation in 1945.

_____

8. Maura (present progressive of *write*) an article on recycling for the newspaper.

_____

9. Descendants of the *Bounty* mutineers (present perfect progressive of *live*) on Pitcairn Island since the eighteenth century.

_____

10. The candidate (past emphatic of *intend*) to visit every state in the Union.

_____

11. "I (future progressive of *test*) you on verb tenses tomorrow," said Mr. Gibbs.

_____

12. Until yesterday Max (past progressive of *plan*) to visit Baffin Island this summer.

_____

Blue Level, Copyright © McDougal, Littell & Company

Voice and Mood

When the subject of a sentence performs the action expressed by the verb, the verb is in the **active voice:** *Dan cooked breakfast.* When the subject receives the action, the verb is in the **passive voice:** *Breakfast was cooked by Dan.*

The **mood** of a verb is the manner in which the verb expresses an idea. The **indicative mood** states a fact or asks a question. The **imperative mood** gives a command or makes a request. The **subjunctive mood** can express a wish or a condition that is contrary to fact. It can also express commands or requests after the word *that.* Subjunctive and indicative verb forms are usually identical, but there are exceptions. Distinctive forms of the subjunctive are as follows:

1. The *s* is omitted from the verb in the third-person singular.
   We asked that she *come* early.
2. The present tense of the verb *to be* is always *be.*
   "If music *be* the food of love, play on." Shakespeare.
3. The past tense form of the verb *to be* is always *were.*
   If I *were* you, I wouldn't watch so much TV.

A. Identifying Active and Passive Voice.
Underline each verb. In the blank, identify the voice of the verb as **active** or **passive.**

1. The meal was prepared by Julia Child. _____

2. The stars have always fascinated people. _____

3. Fruit crops in Florida were destroyed by the cold weather. _____

4. John Philip Sousa wrote "The Stars and Stripes Forever." _____

5. The Denver Broncos won the game. _____

6. The elephant is the only animal with four knees. _____

7. A speech was delivered by the secretary of the student council. _____

8. Several antique cars were owned by the eccentric millionaire. _____

9. This food was donated by schoolchildren.

B. Identifying Moods of Verbs
In the blank, write the mood of the boldfaced verb: **indicative, imperative,** or **subjunctive.**

1. If I ***were*** you, I would write a letter to the editor. _____

2. ***Send*** me a postcard from Seattle. _____

3. The teacher asked that Marty ***complete*** the paper tonight. _____

4. In May of 1983, a severe earthquake ***shook*** Japan. _____

5. Please ***tell*** me what you think of *April Morning*. _____

6. ***Did*** you ***finish*** the report on time? _____

A. identifying Mood

In the blank following each sentence, write **indicative**, **imperative**, or **subjunctive** to identify the mood of the boldfaced verb.

Example   He asked that we *finish* the work in his absence. **subjunctive.**

1. Please *show* me to my seat.   _____

2. The fire *started* at about midnight.   _____

3. *Did* the Civil War *begin* in 1860?   _____

4. "*Play* it again, Sam" was not exactly what Bogart said.   _____

5. He *opened* the garage door carefully.   _____

6. If I *were* governor, I would reduce taxes.   _____

7. Kindly *take* the child's hand.   _____

8. John asked that his name *be* removed from the mailing list.   _____

9. His coaches recommend that he *spend* more time practicing.   _____

10. *Write down* your address and phone number.   _____

11. *Have* you ever *seen* a production of *Hamlet?*   _____

12. I wish I *were* a concert pianist.   _____

B. Using the Active and Passive Voice

You can make the following description of the Hubbard Glacier more lively by changing the verbs that are in the passive voice to the active voice. On the lines below, rewrite the numbered sentences in the active voice. Add words where necessary.

The Hubbard Glacier is grinding to a stop at the head of the Yakutat Bay. **(1)** The mouth of the bay is being closed by the glacier. **(2)** Animals inside the bay are being trapped by the ice flow. **(3)** When the glacier moved, a roaring sound was heard by people. The trapped water was gushing out. **(4)** Ice and debris were carried away by the water. **(5)** The waves from the rushing water were estimated by some onlookers to be thirty feet high.

1. _____

2. _____

3. _____

4. _____

5. _____

Commonly Confused Verbs

Three pairs of verbs are commonly confused: *lie, lay; sit, set;* and *rise, raise.* The definitions and principal parts of these verbs are as follows:

Verb	Definition	Principal Parts
lie	to be horizontal or in a certain place	lie, lying, lay, lain
lay	to set down or put	lay, laying, laid, laid
sit	to be in a seated position	sit, sitting, sat, sat
set	to place or put	set, setting, set, set
rise	to go to a higher position	rise, rising, rose, risen
raise	to lift, to make something go up	raise, raising, raised, raised

Identifying the Correct Verb

Underline the verb in parentheses that correctly completes each sentence.

1. Ms. Diamond's keys were (lying, laying) on the front seat of the car.

2. During evaporation, water vapor (rises, raises) into the air.

3. Wendy always (sits, sets) down on the piano bench to practice when she gets home from school.

4. Tanya (lay, laid) a hand on my arm and said, "Shh."

5. Luis (sat, set) eight begonia plants on the windowsill.

6. The weather forecaster said that the temperature has (risen, raised) during the last

   two hours.

7. Please (lie, lay) those clothes on the ironing board.

8. Mount St. Helens had (lain, laid) dormant since 1857 when it suddenly erupted in 1980.

9. When "Boomer" Jones (rises, raises) his voice, people listen!

10. Let's (sit, set) in front of the fire and discuss this problem.

11. Uncle Calvin had (laid, lain) his cane across the rocking chair.

12. Aunt Lily has (rised, raised) four children and innumerable horses.

13. The phone rang just as we were (sitting, setting) down to dinner.

14. The island group called the Falklands (lies, lays) off the coast of Argentina.

15. The doctor's diagnosis (rose, raised) our hopes considerably.

16. The police officers surprised the mugger as he (laid, lay) in wait for his victim.

17. Abe's father has (set, sat) on two juries in five years.

18. The students (rose, raised) when the famous professor entered.

19. Alexandra was (laying, lying) the paper on the table when she saw the startling headline.

20. I have always (sat, set) high standards for myself.

Commonly Confused Verbs

A. Using Commonly Confused Verbs

Prepare a list of instructions for young children who are learning how to set the table and how to behave at the table. Supply the correct verb in the appropriate form: *lie, lay; sit, set; rise, raise.*

1. _____ the lid of the linen chest.

2. _____ a tablecloth and the napkins on the table.

3. Watch out for the dog _____ under the table.

4. _____ the plates on the tablecloth.

5. _____ the forks on the napkins.

6. You may _____ at the table if you behave politely.

7. You may _____ down after the hostess is seated.

8. Don't _____ your voice during the meal.

9. If the dog bothers anyone, tell it to _____ down.

10. You may _____ from your seat after the hostess does.

B. Using Commonly Confused Verbs

Write a list of instructions for a scavenger hunt or other party game. Tell your guests what they will be doing, where they will be going, and what materials they might need. Your list of directions should include the verb pairs *lie, lay; sit, set;* and *rise, raise.*

_____

_____

_____

_____

_____

_____

_____

_____

_____

_____

Agreement in Number

The **number** of a word indicates whether the word is singular or plural. A word is **singular** in number if it refers to one person or thing and **plural** if it refers to more than one person or thing. The subject (a noun or a pronoun) and verb of a sentence must agree in number; this harmony between subject and verb is called **agreement.** Except for *be,* verbs show a difference between singular and plural only in the third person of the present tense. The third-person-singular present form ends in *s.*

I, you, we, they *talk*   he, she, it *talks*

The verb *be* has special forms for present and past tense in all three persons.

	Present Tense		Past Tense	
	Singular	**Plural**	**Singular**	**Plural**
First Person	I am	we are	I was	we were
Second Person	you are	you are	you were	you were
Third Person	he, she, it is	they are	he, she, it was	they were

Identifying Agreement in Number

In each sentence, underline the verb that agrees in number with the subject.

1. New Zealand (produces, produce) a surplus of meat and dairy products.

2. When the dentist (drills, drill) my teeth, I try to think of pleasant things.

3. Sarah (commutes, commute) to her suburban school from the city center.

4. The skin of an elephant (weights, weigh) over a ton.

5. Where (was, were) you born?

6. Horses (runs, run) one and one quarter miles in the Kentucky Derby.

7. They (was, were) both members of the winning team.

8. Virginia Woolf (is, are) the author of *To the Lighthouse.*

9. The Volta River (meets, meet) the sea on the south coast of Ghana.

10. Adult giraffes (grows, grow) to be about eighteen feet tall.

11. Do you (intends, intend) to go hiking on the Appalachian Trail this summer?

12. Columbia University (awards, award) the Cabot Prize for excellence in inter-
    American journalism.

13. He (reads, read) Art Buchwald's column in the newspaper every week.

14. The President (appoint, appoints) justices to the Supreme Court.

15. Grunions (is, are) small, silvery fish that live along the coast of California.

16. We (visits, visit) the Miami Seaquarium whenever we are in Florida.

17. William Walker's painting *Wall of Love* (expresses, express) the artist's frustration
    with society.

18. As part of the class, you (writes, write) a paper on Mark Twain's novels.

19. The books (was, were) misplaced by your neighbor.

20. Your friends (holds, hold) after-school jobs.

Agreement in Number

A. Making Subjects and Verbs Agree

In each blank write the correct present tense form of the verb in parentheses.

1. The narwhal never (fail) _____ to intrigue people.

2. Because of the long tusk on the male, this small whale (be) _____ often called the "sea unicorn."

3. What narwhals (use) _____ their tusks for is not known.

4. Maybe the narwhal (root) _____ up food from the ocean bottom.

5. Some scientists (think) _____ that the tusk is simply a secondary male characteristic, like the lion's mane.

6. The narwhal (be) _____ hunted by the Eskimos of Greenland.

7. Narwhal meat (contain) _____ abundant vitamins.

8. This creature's tusks (be) _____ no longer used by the Eskimos for harpoon shafts and tent poles.

B. Using Subject and Verb Agreement in Writing

Rewrite the paragraph below, making sure that all subjects and verbs agree.

The acronym *laser* stand for "light amplification by stimulated emission of radiation." Theodore H. Maiman's ruby laser were the first of these devices. A laser differ from fluorescent light or the sun. Lasers has a narrow light beam that is highly directional. Laser light vibrate at only one or very few frequencies. Other light sources has many frequencies. Laser beams cuts steel and fabric, reads supermarket labels, transmit television signals, and carry voice messages. In military operations laser beams bounces off a target and give information about speed and distance of moving objects.

_____

_____

_____

_____

_____

_____

_____

_____

Blue Level, Copyright © McDougal, Littell & Company

Words Between Subject and Verb

A **verb** agrees only with its subject. Occasionally, a word or group of words with a number different from that of the subject comes between the subject and the verb. Even though another word may be closer to the verb than the subject is, the verb must still agree in number with its subject.

> The blouse with the embroidered flowers *is* in the closet.
> Alex, along with his cousins, *is painting* the barn.

A. Making Subjects and Verbs Agree

Underline the subject of each sentence; then underline the verb that agrees with it.

1. Twenty members of the marching band (has, have) arrived for practice.

2. The students, along with their art teacher, (is, are) going to the exhibition.

3. Jennifer, as well as many other tourists, (waits, wait) to kiss the Blarney Stone.

4. Paavo Nurmi, who held twenty world running records, (was, were) known everywhere as "the Flying Finn."

5. Five puppies, together with their champion mother, (was, were) at the dog show.

6. That puzzle, found in both newspapers, (poses, pose) difficult anagrams.

7. Peter Pan, one of Barrie's characters, (runs, run) away to the Neverland.

8. The sale of cassette tapes (has, have) risen in the last year.

9. The decisions of the judge (comes, come) as no surprise. _____

10. Dark nimbus clouds in the summer sky often (foretells, foretell) a thunderstorm. _____

B. Using Subject and Verb Agreement

Cross out each verb that does not agree in number with the subject. Write the correct form of the verb in the blank.

1. The architect's report, along with some models, were presented yesterday. _____

2. Our commander, together with seven officers, want a settlement. _____

3. Houses on that hillside looks very unstable. _____

4. Assistance for the homeless are a long time coming. _____

5. The sheep that graze on the hillside crops the grass very thin. _____

6. The area between France and Spain are mountainous. _____

7. The first steam engine to run on rails were *Puffing Billy*. _____

8. Billy Bishop, one of the most famous World War I pilots, were awarded the Victoria Cross for valor. _____

9. Killdeer, members of the plover family, feigns injury for protection. _____

10. The box, a slow-growing evergreen shrub, grow as high as twenty feet. _____

Words Between Subject and Verb

A. Making Subjects and Verbs Agree
Rewrite each sentence, making the subject and verb agree.

1. John's father, with three other people from the neighborhood, commute to the city each day.

   _____

2. That show, as well as many other musicals, are being performed in the summer theater.

   _____

3. Giacometti's sculpture, along with his paintings and prints, express a feeling of anonymity and helplessness.

   _____

4. Mt. Rushmore, with its sixty-foot-high faces of four Presidents, are a popular tourist attraction.

   _____

5. Wale's coal-mining region, as well as most of its industrial cities, are located in the southern part of the country.

   _____

B. Using Subject and Verb Agreement in Writing
Rewrite this paragraph, making sure all subjects and verbs agree.

   The diamond, along with rubies and emeralds, are one of the world's most precious jewels. Diamonds, in addition to serving as traditional engagement rings, is also used to cut and grind metal. Imperfectly formed diamonds, together with those that contain a flaw, is set in drills used for building automobile and airplane engines. These remarkable jewels, with the hardness of steel, is also found at the end of most record-player needles.

   _____

   _____

   _____

   _____

   _____

   _____

Compound Subjects

Use a plural verb with most compound subjects joined by *and*.

Pauline and Lucy *enjoy* their ballet classes.

Use a singular verb with a compound subject joined by *and* that is habitually used to refer to a single thing.

Cheese and crackers *is* a favorite snack food in our family.

Use a singular verb with a compound subject that is preceded by *each, every,* or *many a.*

Every book and magazine *has* to be checked out at the main desk.

When the words in a compound subject are joined by *or* or *nor,* the verb agrees with the subject nearer the verb.

Either one large scholarship or two smaller ones *are* to be awarded at graduation.
Neither my cleats nor my mitt *is* in my locker.

Using Verbs with Compound Subjects
In each sentence, underline the verb that agrees in number with the subject.

1. Bolivia and Paraguay (is, are) the only landlocked countries in the Americas.

2. Either the ballerina or her students (works, work) in this studio.

3. Every computer and typewriter in the office (was, were) in use.

4. Some doctors believe that either a shot or special nose drops (protects, protect) us from flu viruses.

5. Bacon and eggs (is, are) a high-cholesterol breakfast.

6. Neither the newspapers nor the reporter (has, have) told the true story.

7. Many a novel and short story (reflects, reflect) the author's personal life.

8. Female gnus and their babies (lives, live) in herds on the African plains.

9. Neither my friend Sarah nor I (am, are) pleased about our vacation date.

10. Either Tiffany or her parents (attend, attends) these meetings every week.

11. Neither the city councilors nor the mayor (supports, support) the proposal.

12. Many a problem and worry (vanishes, vanish) with a good night's sleep.

13. Neither the doctor nor the nurses (has, have) seen a similar case.

14. In my opinion, neither Bob nor the pollsters (was, were) correct.

15. Either the clerks or their supervisor (knows, know) how to find the key.

16. Each student (has, have) the option of taking an art class.

17. Every rainstorm and ice storm (is, are) adding to the erosion of the road.

18. Many a swimmer and surfer (has, have) had to be rescued from the rough waters.

19. Neither flurries nor sleet (is, are) predicted for tonight.

20. Peaches and cream (is, are) on the menu.

Compound Subjects

A. Using Verbs with Compound Subjects

In each sentence, underline the verb that agrees in number with the subject.

1. Lox and bagels (is, are) my favorite breakfast.

2. Either Mary or the twins (takes, take) the car to school each day.

3. Its ferocious appearance and its three-foot length (makes, make) the moray eel daunting to encounter under water.

4. Many a toddler and young child (learns, learn) about hot stoves the hard way.

5. Each tremor and small earthquake (makes, make) some Californians nervous.

6. Neither the new students nor Dan (has, have) to take the math test today.

7. Every bush and plant in the garden (is, are) heavy with frozen snow.

8. Either the Markhams or Theresa (walks, walk) past our house every morning.

9. Its long legs and neck and its gray-blue color (identifies, identify) that bird as a great blue heron.

10. Neither the students nor their teacher (has, have) seen *Hamlet* before.

B. Using Compound Subjects in Writing

Rewrite the paragraph below, making all verbs agree in number with their compound subjects.

> Car exhaust fumes and factory smoke pollutes our air. Trees, buildings, and our water supply suffers the effects of pollutants. Every forest and orchard are subject to the effect of acid rain. Smoke and ashes from bonfires creates unclean air. Either decaying leaves or leached water often create pollutants that destroy nutrients in the soil. Neither laws nor regulations totally controls pollution; voluntary measures do make a difference.

_____

_____

_____

_____

_____

_____

_____

_____

Indefinite Pronouns as Subjects

The indefinite pronouns *anyone, each, every, everyone, nobody, no one, nothing,* and *someone* are always singular and take a singular verb. Other singular indefinite pronouns include *anybody, anything, everybody, everything, much, neither, one,* and *somebody.*

> Everyone *was invited* to the reception for the retiring teacher.

The indefinite pronouns *both, few, many,* and *several* are always plural and take a plural verb.

> Several in the class *plan* to become engineers.

The indefinite pronouns *all, any, enough, more, most, none, plenty,* and *some* may be either singular or plural. They take a singular verb when they refer to one thing and a plural verb when they refer to more than one thing.

> Most of the snow *has* now disappeared.
> Most of the books in the limited edition *were* autographed by the author.

Using Correct Agreement

In each sentence, underline the verb that agrees in number with the subject.

1. Many of the seniors (works, work) in order to pay their car insurance.

2. Nothing (alters, alter) the result of our last examination.

3. Several of our friends (is, are) meeting at the wrestling tournament.

4. There (is, are) plenty of deer in a nearby forest preserve.

5. Each of the ducks (is, are) being tagged to trace its migration pattern.

6. Neither of these hats (suits, suit) you.

7. Many in the club (is, are) planning to go on the mystery trip.

8. Both of the vases on the shelf (was, were) made in China.

9. None of the editorials (has, have) changed my father's views.

10. Most of the neighborhood (is, are) participating in the block party.

11. On a hot day, nothing (tastes, taste) so good as a cold fruit salad.

12. Enough of the residents (has, have) signed the petition already.

13. Few of the ski runs (requires, require) as much skill as this one.

14. Some of the dancers (prefers, prefer) jazz dancing to ballet.

15. All of the pieces in the Ramesses exhibit (is, are) over three thousand years old.

16. None of the home games (is, are) televised.

17. Plenty of the sandwiches (was, were) left to provide another meal.

18. Nobody in our class (has, have) ever been to Alaska.

19. Much of Al's coin collection (was, were) lost in the fire.

20. Some of the lawn (has, have) been overwatered.

21. Many of the suits (was, were) on sale, but few (was, were) appealing.

22. Most of the jewelry diamonds (comes, come) from South Africa.

Indefinite Pronouns as Subjects

A. Using Correct Agreement

In each sentence, underline the verb that agrees in number with the subject.

1. Most of Saudi Arabia (consists, consist) of dry, barren land.

2. Unlike the planets, few of the planetary satellites (has, have) an atmosphere.

3. No one (sees, see) the Austrian Alps without being impressed by their beauty.

4. Some of the trains (runs, run) on electricity.

5. Nobody in those classes (knows, know) about the schedule change.

6. Some of the animal life we studied (lives, live) on land.

7. Many of the crew members (has, have) experience sailing in tropical storms.

8. Most of the marshland areas (is, are) a wildlife preserve.

9. Everyone in that class (reads, read) James Thurber's story "The Macbeth Murder Mystery" at the beginning of the year.

10. Each of the team members (gets, get) a chance to take batting practice.

11. Many of the towns and villages in Alaska (has, have) airstrips for small planes.

12. All of those movies directed by Bill Forsythe (has, have) included the beautiful scenery of Scotland.

13. Several of these dogs (makes, make) good guide dogs.

14. Neither of the boys (owns, own) a computer.

15. All of the broadcasts (was, were) aired after the press conference.

B. Using Indefinite Pronouns as Subjects

Rewrite each of these sentences, correcting any errors in subject-verb agreement.

1. Everyone in these pictures are grinning foolishly. _____

_____

2. A few of this kind of flower is included in every bouquet. _____

_____

3. All of the girls and some of the boys swims daily. _____

_____

4. Do anyone among you know the capital of Albania? _____

_____

5. None of the water in the neighboring towns were drinkable. _____

_____

Inverted Sentences

In most sentences, the subject appears before the verb. In **inverted sentences,** this order is reversed. When the subject follows the verb, you must look ahead to the subject to decide whether the verb is to be singular or plural. Problems in agreement often occur in inverted sentences beginning with *here* and *there,* in questions beginning with *who, why, where,* and *what,* and in inverted sentences beginning with a phrase.

> Here *is* an atlas of Australia together with a guidebook.
> There *are* two leaders in this race.
> What *were* the British doing during the Boston Tea Party?
> From this play *come* the characters Puck and Bottom.

A. Identifying the Subject in Inverted Sentences
Underline the subject in each of these inverted sentences.

1. Where is the copy of the original Magna Carta?

2. On the computer is a program that plots maps and graphs.

3. Here are the messages that were sent from New England.

4. Why, given the fine weather, are you still indoors?

5. What are the subjects of these sentences?

6. There is a wasp that actually stings bees.

7. Near the Thames in London is the monument commemorating the Great Fire.

8. There, with all the volleyball team, sits the coach.

9. Coming through the mountain pass was a lonely piper.

10. Who is the person in charge of the meeting?

B. Using Verbs Correctly in Inverted Sentences
In each sentence, underline the verb that agrees in number with the subject.

1. What (is, are) the price of those CB radio kits?

2. On that cushion (sits, sit) the dog and the cat.

3. There (comes, come) a time when we should consider our talents and interests and set certain goals.

4. Here in this package (is, are) your secret documents.

5. In the swamp at the edge of the lagoon (grows, grow) mangrove trees.

6. Where (is, are) the book of photographs by Ansel Adams?

7. What, given your interest in riding trains, hiking, and sailing, (is, are) your vacation plans?

8. Down on our farm (lives, live) sheep, goats, cows, horses, and chickens.

9. Over there among the flower pots (stands, stand) a Grecian urn.

10. Who (is, are) the main characters in Gilbert and Sullivan's *Pirates of Penzance?*

Inverted Sentences

Using Verbs Correctly in Inverted Sentences

In each sentence, underline the verb that agrees in number with the subject.

1. Here (is, are) the acrylic paints for your art project.

2. Presented in this chapter (is, are) five good reasons for learning a foreign language.

3. From Canada (comes, come) some of the racers in the annual Soap Box Derby.

4. (There's, There are) three books on that subject in the library.

5. Why (does, do) Switzerland have three official languages?

6. Through which cities (does, do) the Volga River flow?

7. Here (is, are) the blueprint for the electrical system.

8. Why (has, have) linguists never been able to determine the origin of the Basque language?

9. In Stratford-upon-Avon (stands, stand) statues of Shakespeare's characters Hamlet, Prince Hall, Falstaff, and Lady Macbeth.

10. In what novel (does, do) the characters Ishmael and Captain Ahab appear?

11. Who (is, are) the composers of the operetta *The Yeomen of the Guard?*

12. There (is, are) four cities in Scotland with populations of more than 100,000.

13. Down from the Rocky Mountains (blows, blow) a warm, dry wind called a chinook.

14. In what state (does, do) active volcanoes still erupt?

15. Why (is, are) the giant panda protected by law in China?

16. There (is, are) many cultural, educational, and scientific institutions that were established by grants from Andrew Carnegie.

17. Here (is, are) the thesaurus and the dictionary.

18. Out of the thick fog on the mountain road (appears, appear) the headlights of the oncoming car.

19. Near the German border (lies, lie) the Swiss industrial town of Basel.

20. Over a course of 42.2 kilometers (runs, run) the determined marathoner.

21. (What's, What are) some of the causes of amnesia?

22. In from the east (rolls, roll) the storm clouds.

23. Across the bay, from San Francisco to Sausalito, (extends, extend) the Golden Gate Bridge.

24. What (is, are) the sweaters that Irish fishermen wear called?

25. From the mouth of the volcano (was, were) flowing molten lava.

26. (There's, There are) a small boy and his father at the door.

27. Where (is, are) the painting of Mona Lisa and the statue of Venus de Milo?

28. How (is, are) Todd and his brother training their pet llama?

Other Agreement Problems

There are other situations in which problems in subject-verb agreement arise. When a sentence contains a predicate nominative, the verb agrees in number with the subject, not the predicate nominative.

> The captain's hobby is computers. (*Hobby* is the subject and takes a singular verb.)

In the words *don't* and *doesn't,* the *n't* stands for *not* and is an adverb; it is not part of the verb. Use *don't* with plural subjects and with the personal pronouns *I, we, you,* and *they.* Use *doesn't* with singular subjects and with the personal pronouns *he, she,* and *it.*

Using Verbs That Agree with Their Subjects

In each sentence, underline the verb that agrees in number with the subject.

1. One of Ireland's largest exports (is, are) chemicals.
2. The Ellis twins (is, are) our best hope for a medal in gymnastics.
3. (Doesn't, Don't) the wind in the trees sound fierce tonight?
4. An essential ingredient in mayonnaise (is, are) eggs.
5. His concern (is, are) environmental issues.
6. That law (doesn't, don't) prohibit my dog from walking here.
7. The students' biggest problem (is, are) lack of sleep and too many interests.
8. The staple diet of many Third World inhabitants (is, are) grains.
9. (Doesn't, Don't) the oleander belong to the dogbane family?
10. One of the best buys at the sports shop (is, are) tennis racquets.
11. (Doesn't, Don't) towering oak trees grow from tiny acorns?
12. Agility and flexibility (is, are) his competitive edge.
13. (Doesn't, Don't) our parents' lawyers practice here?
14. The edible part of corn (is, are) the kernels.
15. Her only equipment (was, were) a hammer, a chisel, and some pliers.
16. Mrs. McArthur's collection (is, are) antique dolls.
17. What (doesn't, don't) you like about this meal?
18. The most destructive element of a hurricane (is, are) high winds.
19. Photographs of the construction site (is, are) part of her class project.
20. His main worry during the flood (were, was) his parents.
21. Her children (was, were) her main reason for working.
22. The cause of the fire (was, were) some exposed electric wires.
23. (Doesn't, Don't) fish bite best in early morning?
24. Our cat's main problem (is, are) the three dogs next door.
25. The moral of the two stories (was, were) to persevere in adversity and to have the courage to express one's opinion.

Other Agreement Problems

A. Using Verbs That Agree with Their Subjects
In each sentence, underline the verb that agrees in number with the subject.

1. Painting portraits (was, were) both his hobby and his career.

2. The first prize for the essay contest (is, are) two trips to Washington, D.C.

3. Are you sure it (doesn't, don't) matter which route we take?

4. Noodles, spaghetti, and macaroni (is, are) all pasta.

5. The doctor's prescription (was, were) more rest and a better diet.

6. (Doesn't, Don't) Julie play in our local symphony orchestra?

7. The two sacks (was, were) a heavy load.

8. (Doesn't, Don't) the Cascade Range include Mt. Rainier?

9. The estate he inherited (was, were) a house, a barn, and forty acres.

10. The only food eaten by the koala (is, are) the leaves and buds of the eucalyptus.

11. Uncle Ken's favorite pastime (is, are) reading mysteries.

12. (Doesn't, Don't) it look like rain today?

13. (Doesn't, Don't) each of the players have a chance at bat?

14. Creating musical compositions and playing the piano (relax, relaxes) Trudy.

15. (Doesn't, Don't) Steve and Ed ever go bowling?

16. My chief support (is, are) my mother and my father.

17. The decision of the twelve jury members (doesn't, don't) seem fair.

18. (Doesn't, Don't) Hilda and Marjorie ever wear the pins I gave them?

19. The last people in line (was, were) the French class.

20. The marines on duty (don't, doesn't) get a chance to eat regularly.

B. Using Verbs Correctly in Writing
Rewrite this paragraph, correcting any errors in subject-verb agreement.

> The clothes people wear has often been a sign of social rank or status. An early example are shoes. In ancient Rome, one sign of a woman of high rank were the yellow, red, green, or white shoes she wore. Natural-colored shoes was a sign of a lower-class woman. Today, of course, shoe color don't indicate a person's social status.

_____

_____

_____

_____

_____

Nouns with Singular and Plural Forms

Form A

Some nouns may be either singular or plural subjects, depending on their meaning in the sentence. Verbs used with such nouns present special agreement problems.

A **collective** noun names a group of people or things: *jury, crew, herd*. A singular verb is used when the group is acting together as one unit; a plural verb is used when members or parts of the group are acting individually.

Some singular nouns have a plural form: *news, mumps, macaroni*. As subjects these nouns take a singular verb. Other nouns ending in *s* take a plural verb even though they refer to one thing: *scissors, pliers, trousers, congratulations*.

Some nouns that end in *s* may be either singular or plural, depending on their meaning in the sentence: *ethics, economics, civics*. When plural, these words are often preceded by a possessive form or a modifier.

The name of a country or an organization is singular even though it may be plural in form: *the Philippines, the United Nations*.

A. Identifying Correct Subject-Verb Agreement
In each sentence, underline the correct form of the verb.

1. Mathematics, the favorite subject of some students, (has, have) many divisions.
2. The jury in this case (have, has) different opinions about a verdict.
3. My parents (rent, rents) that apartment house on Babcock Street.
4. My family (is, are) planning to spend its vacation in Canada.
5. The West Indies (is, are) a group of islands.
6. Congratulations (is, are) in order after your successful piano recital.
7. The Student Activities Committee (reports, report) to the principal.
8. His business ethics (seems, seem) sharply different from mine.
9. The cast (was, were) discussing their roles in the upcoming play.
10. Pediatrics (has, have) been selected as his area of specialization.
11. Students for Safety (are, is) a new organization at school.
12. The Philippines (separates, separate) the South China Sea from the Pacific Ocean.
13. The crew of the airliner (is, are) departing for Hawaii at noon.
14. The Boy Scouts (was, were) founded in England in 1908.
15. My ethics (doesn't, don't) allow me to condone their actions.

B. Identifying Correct Subject-Verb Agreement in Inverted Sentences
In each sentence, underline the correct form of the verb.

1. There on the front page (was, were) the election news.
2. In what room (is, are) home economics taught?
3. Among the nations attending (is, are) the United States.
4. In what way (is, are) mumps treated by doctors today?
5. Here on the workbench (is, are) the pliers.

Nouns with Singular and Plural Forms

A. Using Nouns with Singular and Plural Forms

In each sentence, underline the verb that agrees in number with the subject.

1. What (is, are) the latest news about the flood?

2. A flock of Canadian geese often (flies, fly) in a V-shaped formation.

3. The team (disagree, disagrees) about the best strategy.

4. That couple (has, have) moved into the house on Elm Street.

5. The symphony (are, is) practicing individually for the May performance.

6. A herd of wild horses (was, were) grazing in the valley.

7. Ethics (is, are) the study of what is right and wrong in human conduct.

8. Brian's ethics (makes, make) him a man you can trust.

9. For a brilliant performance, the ballet corps (is, are) receiving a warm response from the audience.

10. Aerobics (is, are) a strenuous form of exercise.

B. Using Nouns with Singular and Plural Forms in Writing

Rewrite this paragraph, correcting any errors in subject-verb agreement.

> Our class have been studying the Galápagos Islands, an archipelago in the Pacific. Belonging to Ecuador, the group of islands straddle the equator some 650 miles west of the mainland. The Enchanted Isles were once their name. Discovery of the Galápagos were accidental. In 1535 the Bishop of Panama was searching for fresh water and landed there. Three hundred years later, valuable statistics on the Galápagos finches was obtained by Charles Darwin. Today, any crew of visiting scientists find abundant wildlife, including iguanas, brown pelicans, and flightless cormorants, inhabiting the volcanic islands.

_____

_____

_____

_____

_____

_____

_____

_____

The title of a book, play, short story, film, TV program, musical composition, or other work of art is singular even though it may be plural in form. It therefore requires a singular verb. Use a singular verb with any group of words that refers to a single thing or thought.

> *Bell, Book, and Candle,* I believe, *is* the title of that play.
> "Swedes" *is* a poem by Edward Thomas.
> Where we are *is* a mystery.

Use a singular verb with nouns or phrases that refer to a period of time, a weight, a measurement, a fraction, or an amount of money. Use a plural verb when the subject is a period of time or an amount that is thought of as a number of separate units.

> Two dollars *is* the price. (thought of as a whole)
> Two dimes *have fallen* out of her purse. (thought of as two units)

Using Titles, Groups of Words, Amounts, and Time as Subjects

In each sentence, underline the verb that agrees in number with the subject.

1. "Haste makes waste" (is, are) a familiar saying.

2. One thousand points (is, are) a remarkable score for a beginner.

3. *Wuthering Heights* (is, are) a well-known book by Emily Brontë.

4. Four quarters (was, were) left in the telephone booth.

5. *The Little Foxes* (demonstrates, demonstrate) Lillian Hellman's considerable skill as a playwright.

6. Two pounds of raisins (was, were) the amount used in the recipe.

7. Three weeks (is, are) long enough for a camping trip to the mountains.

8. *Pictures at an Exhibition* (was, were) the last composition on the program.

9. Four yards of fabric (is, are) the total length needed for that dress pattern.

10. After deductions, $204.43 (is, are) my week's wages.

11. How to carve turkeys (was, were) discussed at length.

12. *Two Gentlemen of Verona* (plays, play) at our local theater in March.

13. Seven-eighths of the gas tank (is, are) empty when the warning light flashes.

14. Two hundred twenty yards (equals, equal) one furlong.

15. The 1988 Winter Olympics (was, were) dominated by Eastern European countries.

16. A hundred centimeters (is, are) equivalent to one meter.

17. Picking strawberries (was, were) making our fingers red.

18. Five dollars (was, were) what I still needed for school supplies.

19. Two five-dollar bills (was, were) tucked inside Aunt Rita's card.

20. Richard Armour's *The Classics Reclassified* (retells, retell) some classic tales in a humorous way.

Titles, Groups of Words, Amounts, and Time

A. Using Titles, Groups of Words, Amounts, and Time as Subjects
In each sentence, underline the verb that agrees in number with the subject.

1. *Old Times* by Harold Pinter (is, are) one of his later plays.
2. "Little strokes fell great oaks" (is, are) among the maxims of Benjamin Franklin.
3. Ninety-two miles per hour (was, were) the highest wind speed of the hurricane that hit here last year.
4. Eighteen dollars, the sale price, (seems, seem) reasonable for that sweater.
5. Three weeks (is, are) the time allotted for preparing our research papers.
6. Two miles (is, are) the distance Colleen jogs every morning.
7. Three cups filled with flour (was, were) waiting on the table.
8. Five and a half yards (equals, equal) one rod.
9. Bicycling to and from school five days a week (is, are) Jeremy's fitness program.
10. Roger Kahn's *The Boys of Summer* (is, are) more than just a book about the world of baseball.

B. Using Titles, Groups of Words, Amounts, and Time in Writing
Rewrite this paragraph, correcting any errors in subject-verb agreement.

The Thames, England's longest river, flow from the Cotswolds to the sea. Two hundred fifteen miles are the distance from its source to its mouth. Over three-quarters of the river is nontidal. Above the first locks at Teddington meander the curving Thames. *Three Men in a Boat,* one of Jerome K. Jerome's classics, are set on these upper reaches. Old Father Thames also provide a home for the characters in *The Wind in the Willows.* "In the time of wild roses" are the beginning of a poem about leisure on the Thames.

_____

_____

_____

_____

_____

_____

_____

_____

_____

Relative Pronouns as Subjects

A **relative pronoun** stands in place of its antecedent (the word to which it refers). If the antecedent is plural, the relative pronoun is plural. If the antecedent is singular, the relative pronoun is singular. The verb of the adjective clause introduced by the relative pronoun also agrees in number with the pronoun's antecedent.

> Ann is the student *who is* the valedictorian. (*student* is singular)
> Several students *who have come* close are disappointed. (*students* is plural)

A. Identifying Relative Pronouns and Their Antecedents

In each sentence, underline the relative pronoun and place parentheses around its antecedent. Identify the relative pronoun by writing **singular** or **plural** in the blank.

1. Ireland, which is one of the British Isles, is called *Eire* in Gaelic. _____

2. An acronym is an abbreviation that is also a complete word. _____

3. People who were opposed to slavery were called abolitionists. _____

4. The abacus, which is an ancient counting device, is popular in Asia. _____

5. This is one of the stories that take place in the future. _____

6. Foxes, which belong to the dog family, hunt for food by night. _____

7. An accordion is a musical instrument that works like a reed organ. _____

8. The fossils, which are in the museum, are of an extinct reptile. _____

9. Napoleon I, who was a French military leader, was defeated at Waterloo. _____

10. That is the only one of the strange flowers that has bloomed. _____

B. Using the Correct Verb with a Relative Pronoun

Underline the correct verb in each sentence below.

1. Presidential campaigns often hinge on events that (is, are) not foreseeable.

2. Male peacocks are known for their plumage, which (is, are) quite beautiful.

3. Are these the survivors who (was, were) rescued by the Coast Guard?

4. Sandra Day O'Connor, who (was, were) appointed to the Supreme Court, is the first woman justice on that court.

5. The whale, which (is, are) a mammal with flippers, may once have lived on land.

6. Moss and lichen are two of the dwarf plants that (cover, covers) the tundra.

7. That philodendron is the only one of Pat's plants that (grows, grow) well.

8. Of the two students who (was, were) still in the contest, only Jeff correctly identified the author of *To Kill a Mockingbird*.

9. Caribou are mammals that (lives, live) in the Arctic.

10. Holsteins are the breed of cattle that (gives, give) the most milk.

Relative Pronouns as Subjects

A. Using the Correct Verb with a Relative Pronoun
Underline the correct verb in each sentence below.

1. Good friends are those who (remains, remain) friends through life.
2. Rwanda is one of the African countries that (has, have) suffered from the drought.
3. These are some first day covers that (is, are) worth adding to your stamp collection.
4. Is a conservator a person who (helps, help) restore museum antiques?
5. Sandra is one of those people who (prefers, prefer) Frost's poems to all others.
6. Kevin is the only one in his family who (has, have) many dairy farms.
7. Tipperary, Ireland, is an area that (has, have) many dairy farms.
8. Golfer Lee Trevino has followers who (is, are) known as "Lee's fleas."
9. Tina and Jan are team members who (admires, admire) the coach.
10. Are these the books that (is, are) overdue?

B. Using Relative Pronouns in Writing
Rewrite this paragraph, correcting all errors in subject-verb agreement in the relative clauses.

> Weaving is a craft that have gained popularity in recent years. Weavers from thousands of years ago were unknown artists who has left a legacy of fine art. Examples of their work include blankets, rugs, clothing, baskets, and tapestries, which was made from many natural fibers. Silk, cotton, wool, grasses, rattan, palm leaves, and osiers, all of which was used in weaving, contributed to the art of these craftspeople. Today, some of the weavers who uses these fibers supplement them with synthetic material. Despite mechanization, handloom weaving, which are based largely on traditional designs, continues in many countries.

_____

_____

_____

_____

_____

_____

_____

_____

_____

Directions One or more of the underlined sections in the following sentences may contain errors of grammar, usage, punctuation, spelling, or capitalization. Write the letter of each incorrect section; then rewrite the item correctly. If there is no error in an item, write **E**. Write your answers on your own paper or on an answer sheet, as your teacher directs.

Example   During the 1941 baseball season, Joe DiMaggio hit
                        A   **B**

successfully in 56 straight games: this record has never
                                    C

been broke.   No error
    D   **E**

Answer   D—been broken

1. Two-thirds of the people of Kansas lives in the eastern half of the state; in this
   A   **B**   **C**

   section lay the cities of Kansas City, Wichita, Topeka, and Lawrence.   No error
   D   **E**

2. The song "It Don't Mean a Thing If It Ain't Got That Swing," which Duke Ellington
                                                                          A

   had wrote in 1932, eventually gave the "swing" era its name.   No error
   B   **C**   **D**   **E**

3. Two days before we left Acadia National Park, a ranger had took us on a forest
              A   **B**

   hike to explain the rings made by trees as they add new wood each year.
                                 C   **D**

   No error
   E

4. The *Book of Amazing Facts* describes a phenomenon called "singing dunes,"
                                A

   dunes which make eerie sounds as their grains of sand moves across each other.
         B   **C**   **D**

   No error
   E

5. Neither the elephant nor the rhinoceros are larger than the barrel-shaped
                                            A   **B**   **C**

   hippopotamus, who's name comes from a Greek word for "river horse."   No error
                 D   **E**

6. The New York Times report that during a recent period three-fourths of Texas's
   A   **B**   **C**

   cotton crop were endangered by a long and severe drought.   No error
              D   **E**

7. Hartford, Connecticut, the "Insurance City," became known for reliable insurance
     A   B

   companies in the 1800's; today, about 50 insurance firms have their headquarters
        C   D

   in the city. No error
       E

8. The Black Riders were the first book of poetry by Stephen Crane, the author of the f
    A   B   C

   famous novel "The Red Badge of Courage." No error
        D   E

9. Some of the archaeological team believe that the English monument Stonehenge
            A   B

   was an ancient calendar; however, not one of the archaelogists consider himself
        C   D

   the final authority. No error
        E

10. Up until about 1800, eating tomatoes were considered dangerous; many
     A   B

    Americans back then believed that the juicy fruit, which originated in South
          C   D

    America, was poisonous. No error
         E

11. The supporters of the union have leaded a rally in support of their cause;
           A   B

    every employee and friend were asked to participate. No error
     C   D   E

12. All of the news about the disaster is distressing, but everyone is hoping
     A   B   C

    there will be some good news soon. No error
     D   E

13. During a time of inflation, prices in stores raise as quickly as workers earn
       A   B C   D

    increases in wages. No error
         E

14. Measles is a contagious disease against which most children have been
     A   B   C   D

    inoculated. No error
       E

15. Why do the United States attract so many new immigrants each year, and
      A B   C

    where do most of the new immigrants settle? No error
     D   E

Directions Read the passage and choose the word or group of words that belongs in each numbered space. Write the letter of the correct answer on your own paper or on an answer sheet, as your teacher directs.

Example For a few years around 1910, women ____(1)____ hobble skirts. These skirts were so tight at the bottom that women ____(2)____ hardly walk.

1. A. wear
    B. wore
    C. worn
    D. weared

2. A. could
    B. could not
    C. can
    D. cannot

Answers   1—B   2—A

"Why can't I see it now ____(16)____ asked three-year-old Pamela Land. Her father had just ____(17)____ her photograph, and she didn't want to wait for it to be developed. Walking around the historic village of ____(18)____ Dr. Edwin Land thought about his daughter's question.

The early ____(19)____ a time of rapid advances in Dr. Land's field of research, the physics and chemistry of light. In less than an hour, the scientist devised a plan for the first instant camera. Needless to say, neither Land's daughter nor the rest of the world's photographers ____(20)____ disappointed with Land's new invention.

16. A. ,"
    B. ?"
    C. "?
    D. ",

17. A. take
    B. took
    C. taken
    D. tooken

18. A. Santa Fe, New Mexico
    B. Santa Fe, New Mexico,
    C. Santa Fe, New Mexico.
    D. Santa Fe New Mexico.

19. A. 1940's were
    B. 1940's was
    C. 1940s were
    D. 1940s was

20. A. was
    B. were
    C. are
    D. is

Cases of Pronouns

A **pronoun** is a word that may be used in place of a noun. Pronouns have different forms, or cases, depending on their use in sentences.

	Nominative		Objective		Possessive	
	Singular	**Plural**	**Singular**	**Plural**	**Singular**	**Plural**
First Person	I	we	me	us	my, mine	our, ours
Second Person	you	you	you	you	your, yours	your, yours
Third Person	he she it	they	him her it	them	his her, hers its	their, theirs

A. Identifying the Cases of Pronouns

Underline the pronoun(s) in each sentence. Write **N** above the pronoun to identify nominative case, **O** for objective case, or **P** for possessive case.

1. Don rode his bicycle along the bike path.

2. The performance of flutist James Galway made them cheer.

3. We don't really understand how the human memory works.

4. Give her a chance to speak!

5. My brother and I performed our violin duet with the Santa Fe Opera Company.

6. They warned their patients about the dangers of frostbite.

B. Identifying the Person, Number, and Case of Pronouns

Identify the boldfaced pronoun in each sentence by writing its person (**first, second, third**), number (**S** for singular, **P** for plural), and case (**N** for nominative, **O** for objective, **P** for possessive) in the blank.

> **Example**   Here are the slides from *our* vacation. **first, P, P**

1. The team gave *me* the award for most valuable player. _____

2. The Brooklyn Dodgers did appreciate *their* many loyal fans. _____

3. *She* took photographs of a microscopic animal. _____

4. Many country music fans love Kenny Rogers and *his* music. _____

5. The crowd gave *you* and the band a rousing cheer. _____

6. Juan and *they* tried out for the school play. _____

A. Using Pronouns

Writing without pronouns would be repetitive and awkward. Rewrite each of the numbered sentences in the paragraph below, using pronouns to eliminate repetition. Underline each pronoun you use and label it **N** for nominative, **O** for objective, or **P** for possessive case.

(1) When Thomas Jefferson was President, Jefferson negotiated a large land acquisition from France called the Louisiana Purchase. (2) The next year, in 1804, Lewis and Clark began to explore this vast territory and the Oregon region beyond this territory. (3) Lewis and Clark began Lewis and Clark's journey in St. Louis, Missouri. In traveling through upper Missouri and through the Rocky Mountains, Lewis and Clark were aided by the expedition's only woman, a Shoshone named Sacajawea. (4) Sacajawea's knowledge made Sacajawea an invaluable guide and interpreter. Many dangers confronted these explorers. (5) Americans remember these explorers for daring to explore the unknown.

1. _____

_____

2. _____

_____

3. _____

4. _____

5. _____

B. Using Pronouns in Writing

Write a short paragraph about a historical figure whom you admire. Use pronouns in a variety of ways. Underline the pronouns you use and label them **N** for nominative case, **O** for objective case, and **P** for possessive case.

_____

_____

_____

_____

_____

_____

_____

_____

Pronouns in the Nominative Case

The nominative form of the pronoun is used as a subject of a verb. When a pronoun is part of a compound subject, it is often difficult to decide on the appropriate pronoun form. To decide which pronoun to use in a compound subject, try each part of the subject by itself with the verb.

Mary and *I* went to the tryouts. (Mary went; I went; *not* me went.)

A pronoun that follows a linking verb is called a **predicate pronoun.** A predicate pronoun is in the nominative case.

It was *I* who spoke to you.

Using Pronouns in the Nominative Case

Underline the correct pronoun(s) in each sentence.

1. The Chungs and (I, me) missed the first scene of the play.

2. The cochairpersons of the committee are Harold and (I, me).

3. (They, Them) gave time and money to several charities.

4. The best painters of landscapes in oil are (him, he) and (her, she).

5. Arthur Sullivan and (he, him) wrote many comic operas.

6. That could be (they, them) waiting at the door of the museum.

7. (He, Him) and the Argonauts went on a quest for the Golden Fleece.

8. The person driving the car through the tunnel was (she, her).

9. The prima ballerina of the Bolshoi Ballet is still (her, she).

10. Fred and (me, I) cooked the pancakes for the fund-raising breakfast.

11. It could have been (them, they) who finished first in the mile relay.

12. (They, Them) visited Java, the most densely populated island in Indonesia.

13. I was (he, him) who organized the Boston Tea Party.

14. The person who photographed the sunrise was (I, me).

15. (Him, He) insisted that whales were once land animals.

16. Tom and (she, her) told the class that the fennec is the smallest fox in the world.

17. (We, Us) read that Queen Anne's lace is really a wild white carrot.

18. Was it Pablo and (him, he) who gave the report on Northern Ireland?

19. Our friends and (we, us) are traveling to Spain next summer.

20. You and (them, they) should audition for the regional orchestra.

21. The winners of the essay contest were Sarah and (he, him).

22. Did Degas or (she, her) paint this picture of people at the opera?

23. If it rains, (he, him) or (I, me) will cover the bicycles with canvas.

24. Are you and (we, us) going to be on different teams?

25. The understudy for this role will be James or (he, him).

Pronouns in the Nominative Case

A. Using Pronouns in the Nominative Case
Underline the correct pronoun(s) in each sentence.

1. It was (us, we) whom you heard laughing on the porch last night.

2. Nancy and (I, me) played chess for several hours yesterday.

3. It must have been (her, she) who rang the doorbell.

4. (He, Him) and Laura belong to the debate club and the speech team.

5. It is (us, we) who made the phone call to Halifax.

6. (We, Us) and (they, them) plan to vacation in Big Sur this summer.

7. Bob and (I, me) both know who the culprit was in that film.

8. Humphrey Bogart and (she, her) starred in several films together.

9. You and (I, Me) both know who the culprit was in that film.

10. Was it (they, them) you saw at the volleyball game on Thursday?

11. It may have been either (he, him) or (she, her) who sent the flowers.

12. Will the Democratic candidate for governor be (her, she)?

B. Using Pronouns in the Nominative Case
Fill in the blanks in the sentences following the paragraph with the appropriate pronoun in the nominative case. On the line following the sentence, write the word(s) the pronoun refers to. Base your answers on the information given in the paragraph.

Mimes portray feeling and character through gesture, movement, and facial expression—but not words. The art of mime, or pantomime, descends from a form of ancient Greek and Roman comic entertainment. The ancient Roman mime actors used masks in their performances, relying on gesture to convey feelings. Western mime has been strongly influenced by sixteenth-century Italians and their invention of characters such as the harlequin. In modern times, other countries have expanded the art of mime. The American silent-film actor Charlie Chaplin stretched both the comic and the tragic capacity of mime expression. Marcel Marceau, a well-known French mime, has traveled around the world to share his trademark character, Bip.

1. _____ use gesture, movement, and facial expressions, but not words. _____

2. _____ descends from the ancient Greek and Romans. _____

3. Was it _____ who used masks in mime performances? _____

4. The inventors of the harlequin were _____. _____

5. It was _____ whose talent for both comic and tragic mime was captured

   on film. _____

6. The person who created the character Bip was _____. _____

Pronouns in the Objective Case

Like a noun, a pronoun can function as the object of a verb, the object of a preposition, or part of an infinitive phrase. The **objective** pronoun form is used as a direct or indirect object or as the object of a preposition. To decide which pronoun form to use in a compound object, try each part of the object by itself with the verb or preposition.

> Jan told Rosa and *him* the news. (told Rosa; told him, *not* told he)
> Ilia sang for Jo and *me*. (for Jo; for me, *not* for I)

The objective pronoun form is used as the subject (**S**), object (**O**), or predicate pronoun (**PP**) of an infinitive (**I**).

>   **S   I   O   I PP**
> I told *them to keep her* in their camera sights; I knew the winner *to be her*.

Choosing the Correct Pronoun

Underline the correct pronouns(s) in each sentence.

1. Just between you and (me, I), I'm afraid of flying in an airplane.

2. The money will be divided among the Ortegas, the Wojciks, and (we, **us**).

3. The Mayor presented the Senator and (him, he) keys to the city.

4. Mrs. Barnes asked Julio and (me, I) to help landscape her yard.

5. Mr. Riley, who works at the planetarium, gave Joe and (I, me) a tour.

6. Thank Rolanda and (she, her) for their help in developing the pictures.

7. Reading suspense novels late at night sometimes scares my brother and (I, me).

8. Anita told Leon and (she, her) that there were 66,000 lakes in Finland.

9. There is a message on the desk for (they, them) regarding tonight's rehearsal.

10. The librarian told Carla and (he, him) to look for materials in the vertical file.

11. The instructor asked Juanita and (me, I) several difficult questions.

12. The basketball center towered over Brandon and (me, I).

13. We expected (she, her) to drive (him, he) to the airport.

14. Our aunt sent a letter to Sandy and (I, me).

15. I requested recommendations from Ms. Sanchez and (he, him).

16. Did you ask Nicky and (they, them) to help at the book sale?

17. We wanted the shortstop to be (she, her).

18. The conductor gave the brass section and (we, us) a cue to play softly.

19. Mr. Frost had to excuse (they, them) from taking the exam.

20. Our neighbors threw a party for my sister and (me, I).

21. I gave several of my old books to John and (she, her).

22. We lost the ball to (them, they) in the final quarter.

23. There were only a few yards between (us, we) and the dock.

24. The judges announced the winner to be (he, him).

25. We waited an extra hour for (they, them) and their friends.

Pronouns in the Objective Case

A. Choosing the Correct Pronoun
Underline the correct pronoun(s) in each sentence.

1. The news director told (they, them) to keep (she, her) informed about that story.

2. The judges and we all thought the winner of the long jump to be (he, him).

3. We asked (he, him) and his brother for directions.

4. The misunderstanding troubled both our parents and (we, us).

5. Between (she, her) and (I, me) we were able to carry the table inside.

6. If the phone rings, it will probably be for (she, her) or (he, him).

7. Someone borrowed the tools without the permission of Ms. Davis or (he, him).

8. The pool regulations required my friends and (me, I) to be out by 9:00 P.M.

9. Mr. Kwan asked John to give (her, him) help with this math problem.

10. The small package is from Sally and (me, I).

11. There has been very little communication between Michael and (they, them) lately.

12. We hoped to settle the argument between (we, us) and (they, them).

B. Using Pronouns in the Objective Case
In the following paragraph, find the four sentences with errors in pronoun usage. Revise the sentences on the lines below.

  (1) Our concept of money as dollars and cents is not the only one in the world. **(2)** Between we and England, for example, lies a shared language, but we have different meanings for the word *pound*. **(3)** A Mexican storekeeper dealing with U.S. customers would ask they to change their dollars into pesos first. **(4)** Likewise, a U.S. woman touring India might find that her lack of rupees embarrasses her husband and she. **(5)** If we visited Korea, the Koreans would ask you and I to pay them in won. **(6)** If an Italian gave you several thousand lira, you would have little cause to celebrate, for that amount would be worth only a few dollars in U.S. currency.

_____

_____

_____

_____

_____

_____

_____

Pronouns in the Possessive Case

Personal pronouns that show ownership use the possessive case. Possessive pronouns can replace or modify nouns. The possessive pronouns *mine, ours, yours, his, hers, its,* and *theirs* can be used in place of nouns. The possessive pronouns *my, our, your, his, her, its,* and *their* modify nouns. Notice that *his* and *its* are used in either situation.

This is not *my* notebook; it is *yours.*

The possessive form of the pronoun is used when the pronoun immediately precedes a gerund but not when it precedes a participle. Remember that if the *-ing* word is used as a noun, it is a gerund; if it is used as a modifier, it is a participle.

Our singing thrilled the crowd. (*Singing* is a gerund used as the subject of the sentence. *Our* modifies *singing.*)
He saw me hiking up the hill. (*Hiking* is a participle modifying *me.*)

A. Identifying Pronouns in the Possessive Case
Underline the possessive pronouns(s) in each of the following sentences.

1. Michelangelo's frescoes in the Sistine Chapel may be his greatest accomplishment.
2. Their beauty pays tribute to his unusual gifts as an artist.
3. His painting the huge ceiling required artistic, technical, and physical skill.
4. Michelangelo's sense of space aided his planning of the enormous frescoes.
5. Today workers in the chapel are trying to restore its original beauty.
6. Some art historians and other experts have their doubts about whether some of the shadings that are being cleaned off Michelangelo's work are actually his.
7. Our assumptions about his style in the chapel are being challenged.
8. Still, from his time to ours, Michelangelo has touched millions through his art.

B. Choosing the Correct Possessive Pronoun
Write the correct possessive pronoun in each blank.

1. When a goose is cold, it fluffs up _____ feathers to trap air.
2. When other animals are cold, they bristle _____ hair or fur.
3. This layer of air around an animal helps to preserve _____ body heat.
4. We humans also bristle _____ hair when cold, but _____ is so fine that we can see _____ hair follicles standing up.
5. You might prefer to call _____ own bristling "getting goose bumps."
6. If I compare _____ own natural covering to that of a goose. I can see that _____ is less efficient at trapping air.

Pronouns in the Possessive Case

A. Choosing the Correct Possessive Pronoun
Write the correct possessive pronoun in each blank.

1. Willa Cather's novels reveal _____ gifts of observation.

2. We are told that _____ was a sensibility shaped by _____ leaving Virginia as a young girl for the prairies of Nebraska.

3. In _____ report, I explain how several of Cather's _____ stories of frontier life focus on the intermingling of established American settlers and new emigrants from Europe.

4. She saw that _____ settling the Midwestern plains together created a unique social environment.

5. Cather's writing has enriched _____ understanding of ways of life in the early days of the Midwest and elsewhere.

6. A French priest and _____ coming to terms with life in New Mexico are the subject of her novel *Death Comes for the Archbishop.*

B. Using Pronouns in the Possessive Case
In the following paragraph, find the five sentences with errors in pronoun usage. Revise the sentences on the lines below.

      (1) Cleopatra's reign as queen of Egypt deserves us remembering her as one of the most colorful figures of ancient times. (2) She revolting against her own father won Cleopatra the Egyptian throne. (3) Many men loved her, including the Romans Julius Caesar and Marc Antony. (4) By hers marrying Marc antony, Cleopatra hoped to sustain her empire.
(5) Contrary to Cleopatra's plans, however, hostile Roman forces led to the downfall of Antony and Cleopatra and to them killing themselves in despair.
(6) In him dramatizing Cleopatra's life, Shakespeare joins many writers who have considered her a fascinating character.

_____

_____

_____

_____

_____

_____

_____

Who, Whom, and Whose

Who, whoever, whom and whomever are used to ask questions and to introduce adjective or noun clauses.

Who and whoever are in the nominative case and can act as the subject (S) or predicate pronoun (PP) in a clause.

S	**PP**
Tell me *who* said that.	I'll thank *whoever* it was.

Whom and whomever are in the objective case and can act as the direct object (DO) in a clause or as the object of a preposition (OP).

DO	**OP**
Invite *whomever* you want.	Al is the one for *whom* the card came.

To use *who* and *whom* in questions, it is necessary to understand how the pronoun is functioning in the question.

S	**DO**
Who will be chosen?	*Whom* will you choose?

Whose functions as the possessive pronoun within a clause.

I know *whose* hat that is.

Choosing the Correct Pronouns

Underline the correct pronoun(s) in each sentence.

1. (Who, Whom) do you know in Denver, Colorado?

2. Complete the assignment with (whoever, whomever) you want.

3. Ernest Hemingway, one of many American writers (who, whom) lived in Paris in the 1920's, wrote *The Old Man and the Sea*.

4. Melinda is the player (who, whose) efforts benefited the team.

5. Samantha was the little girl for (who, whom) the story was originally written.

6. (Whoever, Whomever) completes the marathon will be awarded a medal.

7. Geckos are lizards seen by (whomever, whoever) visits the Southwestern deserts.

8. (Who, Whom) wrote *Evangeline?*

9. Carl Sandburg is one of the poets (who, whose) work we studied in English last year.

10. By (who, whom) was the White House first occupied?

11. The new principal will be (whoever, whomever) the school board supports.

12. Alexander asked, "(Who, Whom) did you see at the play?"

13. Someone called, but I don't know (who, whom) it was.

14. I wonder (whose, whom) home-run record Hank Aaron surpassed.

15. The lead singer in the first band to perform, (whoever, whomever) he was, had a sensational voice and great charisma.

Who, Whom, and Whose

A. Using Pronouns Correctly

Choose each sentence with the appropriate pronoun: *who, whom, whoever, whomever,* or *whose.*

1. The librarian _____ sits in the reference area will assist you.

2. Pablo Picasso was the painter _____ we learned most about this term.

3. We wondered _____ short story would win the school prize.

4. Dad wants _____ walked the dog to hang up the leash now.

5. The musician _____ we met plays for the Atlanta Symphony Orchestra.

6. Charelle can ask _____ she wants to be her lab partner.

7. Mr. Knaus asked, "_____ in this class has read *Don Quixote?*"

8. Robert E. Peary and Frederick Cook were two explorers, both of

   _____ claimed to have reached the North Pole first.

9. The composer Mozart, _____ works are performed frequently

   today, died penniless in 1791.

10. "Give this package to _____ answers the door," said Max.

B. Correcting Problems in Pronoun Usage

Find the incorrect pronouns in the numbered sentences below. Write the correct pronoun in the corresponding blank. If the sentence has no error, write **Correct** in the blank.

Who knows why the magnificent Mayan civilization of Central America collapsed over a thousand years ago? **(1)** The Maya, who we credit with achievements in the fields of architecture, astronomy, mathematics, and the arts, peaked as a civilization around A.D. 250. **(2)** The Maya were the people whom understood the movement of the sun and stars better than anyone else at the time. **(3)** They made a calendar whose basis was the 365-day orbit of the earth around the sun. **(4)** The Maya are also the people to who we owe the invention of the zero. **(5)** Whomever sees the inscribed stone monuments in the ruins of their ancient cities is looking at an original system of writing. **(6)** Students, especially those for who history is interesting, will continue to wonder why the Mayan civilization declined.

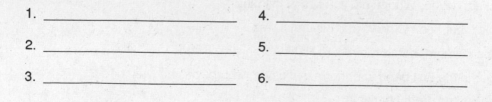

1. _____   4. _____

2. _____   5. _____

3. _____   6. _____

Blue Level, Copyright © McDougal, Littell & Company

Pronouns with Appositives

The pronouns *we* and *us* are often followed by an **appositive,** a noun that identifies the pronoun. To decide whether to use the nominative or objective case, drop the noun and read the sentence without it.

> The manager gave *us* clerks a raise. (gave us, *not* gave we)

Sometimes the pronoun itself is used as an appositive. The form of a pronoun used as an appositive is determined by the function of the noun with which it is in apposition. To decide which form of the pronoun to use in apposition, try the appositive by itself with the verb or preposition.

> The skaters, Brian and *she*, won the gold medal. (she won, *not* her won)
> Tom approached the singers, Ana and *her*. (approached her, *not* approached she)

Choosing the Correct Pronoun

Underline the correct pronoun in each sentence.

1. The class president nominees, Allyssa and (me, I), need your support.

2. Most of (we, us) hockey players like to skate for fun as well as in games.

3. For the two runners, Harriet and (she, her), the conditions were favorable.

4. The response to the movie was very different for each one of us—Kristin, Danielle, Tricia, and (me, I).

5. (We, Us) U.S. citizens celebrate our independence on July 4.

6. The newest members of the Mountain Club, Reggie and (they, them), were introduced at the planning meeting.

7. His cousins, Michelle and (he, him), were meeting their teammates in Portugal.

8. The thunderstorm caught some of (us, we) students on the field.

9. Two schools, East High and (us, we), will compete on College Bowl.

10. First and second place went to the new entrants, the Wilsons and (they, them).

11. (Us, We) seniors are preparing for a class trip to Silver Bay.

12. The seniors in our French class, Joyce and (she, her), have more trouble pronouncing the vocabulary than learning it.

13. Everyone knows that (we, us) musicians are also good at math.

14. Every year the best parts in the class play always go to the two most talented drama students, Melissa and (he, him).

15. "There's no one here except (we, us) volunteers," said Alana.

16. The two best jazz groups, the Grace Notes and (we, us), will represent our school.

17. (We, Us) gymnasts spend several hours a week devising routines.

18. Thousands of (we, us) fans turned out for the team's victory parade.

19. The contestants, John and (me, I), stood alone onstage.

20. The moderator asked the finalists, Eric and (she, her), a final question.

Pronouns with Appositives

A. Using the Correct Pronoun

Rewrite the following sentences, correcting any errors in pronoun usage. If a sentence contains no errors, write **Correct**.

1. The mural on the left was created by all three of us—Allan, Dan, and I.

_____

2. Two of our best hitters, Al and him, made the all-star team.

_____

3. To we tennis players, the closing of the south court was a real disappointment.

_____

4. We chatted with the twins, Rob and she, at the class outing.

_____

5. Us alternates watched the game tensely, hoping to be called in.

_____

6. Even without our two strongest debaters, him and Carla, we came in second in the all-city debating tournament.

_____

_____

B. Correcting Problems in Pronoun Usage

Find the incorrect pronouns in the numbered sentences below. Write the correct pronoun and the noun to which it refers in the corresponding blank. If a sentence has no error, write **Correct** in the blank.

(1) Viewing Saturn in the night sky was an event that us astronomy students had awaited anxiously. (2) We had written to two universities, and with high-powered telescopes from three sources—the planetarium and they—we could see the planet. (3) Us students were awed by the sight of its rings. (4) Four classmates—Nan, Peter, and them—were especially knowledgeable about Saturn; their information only increased our enjoyment of the experience. (5) Both the teacher and us students looked through the instruments time and time again. (6) The telescope brought us earthlings closer to our subject; we returned to class the next day with renewed excitement.

1. _____   4. _____

2. _____   5. _____

3. _____   6. _____

Blue Level   Copyright © McDougal Littell & Company

Other Problems with Pronouns

Comparisons can be made by using a clause that begins with *than* or *as*.

> Sheila reads more *than* I do.

In some cases, the final clause is incomplete, or **elliptical.** To decide which pronoun form to use in an elliptical clause, fill in the missing word(s) to complete the comparison.

> John is taller than *I*. John is taller than *I am.*

A **reflexive pronoun** such as *myself* cannot be used alone. It must refer to a preceding noun or pronoun.

> The hikers suddenly found *themselves* on a ledge.

A. Choosing the Correct Pronoun

In each sentence, underline the correct pronoun.

1. Robin is a better archer than (he, him).

2. Betty wrote a better monologue than (I, myself).

3. Since Mom and Dad were at work, we made lunch for (us, ourselves).

4. Everyone was aboard the train except (themselves, them).

5. Hundreds of fans gave up and left the ticket line before (we, us).

6. Do you think anyone sings as well as (he, him) today?

B. Using Pronouns Correctly

Rewrite the sentences, correcting pronoun errors. If the sentence contains no errors, write **Correct**.

1. The cottontail rabbit dug itself a burrow.

_____

2. She purchased tickets for ourselves so that we could go also.

_____

3. He solved the problem by requesting help from Jake and myself.

_____

4. The Brothers Grimm were certainly better storytellers than him.

_____

5. Except for ourselves, no one attended the meeting.

_____

6. Does this car belong to yourself, or have you borrowed it?

_____

Other Problems with Pronouns

A. Using the Correct Pronoun

Rewrite the following sentences, correcting any errors in pronoun usage. If a sentence contains no errors, write **Correct**.

1. Others had experimented with telegraphic systems before Samuel Morse, but he was ultimately more successful than them.

   _____

   _____

2. Kara and myself intend to visit the science museum on Tuesday.

   _____

3. Although Clara Schumann composed fewer works than her husband, she was as accomplished a musician as him.

   _____

   _____

4. If you are well prepared, the examination will be no more difficult for you than she.

   _____

5. For myself, the second trip to Seattle was as much fun as the first.

   _____

B. Correcting Errors in Pronoun Usage

Find the incorrect pronouns in the numbered sentences. Write the correct pronoun in the corresponding blank. If a sentence contains no errors, write **Correct** in the blank.

   (1) There were many backpackers who were more experienced that me. **(2)** Nevertheless, none could have enjoyed the beautiful sights of Grand Teuton National Park more than myself. **(3)** With its great variety of glaciated canyons and spectacular lakes and peaks, the park made my friends and me forget us. **(4)** I equipped myself with a camera, sure that I could take these spectacular scenes home with me. **(5)** Each of us had special ways of recording the experience for us. **(6)** Anita and I took pictures, Dick kept a journal, and Paula—no one else draws as well as her—made sketches.

1. _____   4. _____

2. _____   5. _____

3. _____   6. _____

Pronoun-Antecedent Agreement

An **antecedent** is the noun or pronoun to which a pronoun refers. A pronoun must agree with its antecedent in person, number, and gender. When a singular indefinite pronoun is the antecedent of another pronoun, the second pronoun must be singular. Singular indefinite pronouns include *anybody, anyone, each, either, everybody, everyone, neither, nobody, no one, one, somebody, someone*.

> *Neither* (singular) of the girls remembered *her* (singular) report.

Singular antecedents joined by *or* or *nor* are referred to by a singular pronoun. Collective nouns may take either a singular or a plural pronoun depending on meaning. When the antecedent is a noun that may be either masculine or feminine, it is acceptable to use the phrase *his* or *her* to refer to it.

> *Either* Damien *or* Jason lost *his* jacket.
> The *jury* disagree with *their* foreman. (Jury members act individually.)
> The *jury* reached *its* decision. (The jury is a unified whole.)
> *Everyone* should hand in *his or her* paper.

A. Identifying Antecedents
In each sentence below, write a **P** over the pronoun and an **A** over the antecedent.

1. The horse threw its rider onto the ground.

2. Freshmen can try out for the debate team if they are so inclined.

3. Sometimes typists place carbon paper in their typewriters to make extra copies.

4. The museum displayed its collection of early Americana.

5. Neither Peter nor Peter's mother can read his sister's handwriting.

B. Making Pronouns and Antecedents Agree
If a boldfaced pronoun does not agree with its antecedent, write the proper pronoun in the blank. If a pronoun agrees with its antecedent, write **Correct**.

1. Several of the photography students entered **his or her** self-portraits in a contest. _____

2. Neither Anton nor Juan wants **their** painting sold at the exhibit. _____

3. Each of the clubs will present **their** own program on Friday. _____

4. The ballet troupe is having **their** picture taken. _____

5. Did anyone claim the book as **theirs?** _____

6. The cast went **their** separate ways when the play ended. _____

7. Ten tourists waited patiently in line for **his or her** tickets. _____

8. Either Annie or Jane will give **their** report today. _____

9. Everyone came up after class to pick up **his or her** tickets. _____

10. Susan and Linette invited me to go fishing on **their** boat. _____

Pronoun-Antecedent Agreement

A. Making Pronouns and Antecedents Agree

Check the boldfaced pronouns to make sure that they agree with their antecedents. If a pronoun does not agree with its antecedent, write the correct pronoun in the blank. If a pronoun agrees with its antecedent, write **Correct**.

1. Everyone found *their* seat again after intermission.   _____

2. Yesterday the Institute of Contemporary Art held a reception to celebrate *their* third anniversary.   _____

3. Has anyone brought *his or her* own lunch?   _____

4. Is the chemistry department satisfied with *their* new facilities?   _____

5. Each passenger is responsible for *their* own luggage.   _____

6. Was it Plato or Aristotle who had Alexander the Great as one of *their* pupils?   _____

7. Charlemagne's court at Aachen was one of the most literate of *their* time.   _____

8. Each of the members of the chorus signed *their* name on the card.   _____

9. Did either Rosencrantz or Guildenstern have a personality of *his* own?   _____

10. Without a good night's sleep, no one can expect to be at *their* best.   _____

11. Has either Emily or Gwen received *their* award yet?   _____

12. The orchestra quickly found *its* place and began to play.   _____

B. Making Pronouns and Antecedents Agree in Writing

Find the incorrect pronoun in each of the numbered sentences. Write the correct pronoun and its antecedent in the corresponding blank.

   (1) Caricature, the art of making satirical portraits, has their roots in seventeenth-century Italy. During the eighteenth century, the comic art of caricature flourished in England in literature as well as in art. **(2)** Neither the artists nor the writers based his caricatures solely on grim reality. Charles Dickens is a famous literary caricaturist. **(3)** Many of Dickens's characters remain in our memories because of his exaggerated appearances and mannerisms. Modern political cartoons are another type of caricature.
(4) Few of these cartoonists want his work to hurt the politician; cartoonists intend only to expose follies and foibles. **(5)** In order to draw a successful caricature, one must train their eye to select the feature that should be exaggerated or distorted.

1. _____   4. _____

2. _____   5. _____

3. _____

Pronoun Reference

To avoid confusion, every personal pronoun should refer clearly to a definite antecedent. The **reference** of a pronoun is indefinite if there is no one word the pronoun clearly refers to. The reference is ambiguous if the pronoun may refer to more than one word.

Avoiding Indefinite and Ambiguous References

Revise the sentences below to correct all indefinite or ambiguous pronoun references.

> **Example**   It says in the book that Elizabeth I was a great queen.
> **The book says that Elizabeth I was a great queen.**

1. The wizard Merlin told the young King Arthur that the sword was his.

   _____

2. Using sonar devices, they are searching for the famous Loch Ness monster.

   _____

3. A finch egg is the size of a marble, and it weighs one gram.

   _____

4. In the preface it explains how they used to live on homesteads in the 1800's.

   _____

5. We removed the pictures from the walls and cleaned them thoroughly.

   _____

6. Jessica took the turtle out of the terrarium and washed it.

   _____

7. In the nineteenth century, you had to work twelve-hour days.

   _____

8. Sam understood the introduction to the *The Scarlet Letter* after he read it.

   _____

9. In some parts of the West, you get very little rainfall.

   _____

10. Bill and Karen unloaded the bags from the shopping carts and returned them.

    _____

Pronoun Reference

A. Avoiding Indefinite and Ambiguous References
Revise the sentences below to correct all indefinite or ambiguous pronoun references.

1. On his bicycle Ken followed the rock star's bus until it broke down. _____

   _____

2. It says in this book that erupting volcanoes can generate lightning. _____

   _____

3. I arranged my plant on the bookshelf, but it still didn't look right. _____

   _____

4. You shouldn't make promises that you can't keep. _____

   _____

5. The coaches worked with the runners until they were satisfied. _____

   _____

B. Using Proper Pronoun References
In the following paragraph, find the five sentences with indefinite or ambiguous pronoun references. Revise the sentences on the lines below.

(1) They often use Harlem as an example of urban poverty. (2) This section of New York City, however, once enjoyed better days. (3) African-American literature and culture flourished during the Harlem Renaissance of the 1920's. (4) Musicians from New Orleans brought jazz to Harlem. (5) Intellectuals flocked to Harlem circles because you had a stimulating atmosphere. (6) Writers and activists such as W. E. B. DuBois argued for full and immediate racial equality. (7) Poets such as Langston Hughes found it meaningful to write about black urban life. (8) As white readers sampled the work of Hughes, Claude McKay, and others, their reputations spread. (9) Its cultural contributions endured long after the Great Depression had caused economic decline in Harlem.

_____

_____

_____

_____

_____

_____

_____

Understanding Modifiers

An **adjective** is a modifier that tells *which one, what kind,* or *how many* about a noun or pronoun. An **adverb** is a modifier that tells *how, when, where,* or *to what extent* about a verb, an adjective, or another adverb. Most adverbs are formed by adding *-ly* to adjectives: *clear/clearly; quick/quickly.*

Always use an adverb to modify an action verb: *She ran quickly.* A linking verb is usually followed by an adjective rather than by an adverb: *That sounds good. He was happy to receive the award.*

Verbs that can be used as both linking and action verbs include *look, sound, appear, grow, smell, taste,* and *remain.* When these verbs are used as action verbs, they can be modified by adverbs.

> The cutting edge *feels* sharp. (linking verb)
> A quality inspector *feels* fabric carefully.

A. Identifying Modifiers Correctly

Underline the word being modified by the boldfaced word. Then, after each sentence, write **ADJ** if the modifier is an adjective and **ADV** if the modifier is an adverb.

1. You can hear the scratches if you listen **carefully** enough. _____

2. Joanna always does her work **quickly** so that she can leave on time. _____

3. The ball was too **high** for the outfielder to catch. _____

4. The samples in the cheese factory smelled very **strong.** _____

5. The boy looked **longingly** at the ten-speed bicycle in the window. _____

6. Attached to the bank of the river, the canoe was bobbing **peacefully.** _____

7. Elena usually speaks **softly.** _____

8. The colors in the forgery were almost **perfect.** _____

B. Choosing the Correct Modifier

Underline the correct modifier in each sentence below.

1. Aaron Copland's musical compositions sound (distinct, distinctly) American.

2. Talc feels (soft, softly), and quartz looks glossy.

3. Sally Ride became (famous, famously) as the first American woman in space.

4. He looked (shy, shyly) in the direction of his older brother.

5. The rains (relentless, relentlessly) eroded the hillside.

6. The music from the auditorium sounded (beautiful, beautifully).

7. They listened to the debate (intent, intently).

8. The sky often grows (calm, calmly) just before a storm.

9. Cyril (quiet, quietly) tiptoed into the room.

10. Between walruses and sea lions, sea lions are more (energetic, energetically).

Understanding Modifiers

A. Choosing the Correct Form of the Modifier

Complete each sentence using the correct form of the word in parentheses. Then, in the blank after each sentence, write **ADJ** if the word you have used is an adjective and **ADV** if the word is an adverb.

1. Fables are stories that offer _____ advice. (useful) _____

2. Some German words _____ resemble related words in English. (close) _____

3. Although some scholars have questioned the signature's authenticity, the leading

   expert believes it is _____. (original) _____

4. John looks _____ at the painting. (intent) _____

5. Sue appears _____ when she reads. (intent) _____

6. The stew she had was _____ and _____. (hot, savory) _____

7. A mathematician must think _____ to solve equations. (logical) _____

8. Her description of undergraduate life at Oxford is _____. (vivid) _____

B. Using Modifiers Correctly

Examine the paragraph below. Underline the modifiers in each sentence once, and underline the modified word twice. Then, in the space above each modifier, identify it as **ADV** (adverb) or **ADJ** (adjective).

(1) The human fascination with flying harks back to the Greek myth of Daedalus and his son Icarus. (2) Daedalus, whose inventions were brilliant, was trapped on the island of Crete. (3) King Minos of Crete ordered him to build a gigantic labyrinth to contain the horrible Minotaur. (4) The Minotaur was fierce and hideous, with the head of a bull and the body of a man.

(5) Then Daedalus unwisely helped the god of the sea, Poseidon, in a plot against Minos. (6) As punishment, King Minos cruelly imprisoned Daedalus and Icarus in the labyrinth. (7) Daedalus' plan of escape seemed clever: he made wings of wax and feathers for himself and Icarus. (8) The wings worked beautifully, but Icarus foolishly disobeyed his father's warning not to exceed a certain height. (9) As Icarus flew sunward, his wings grew hot and began to melt. (10) Daedalus could only watch his son plunge helplessly into the sea.

Comparison of Adjectives and Adverbs

Every adjective and adverb has a basic form called the **positive degree:** Rita is *quick.* The **comparative degree** of an adjective or an adverb is used to compare two things, groups, or actions: Rita is *quicker* than Mae. The **superlative degree** of an adjective or an adverb is used to compare more than two things, groups, or actions: Rita is the *quickest* runner on the team.

Most one-syllable modifiers form the comparative and superlative degrees of comparison by adding *-er* and *-est* to the positive degree: *clearer, clearest.* (Some two-syllable words also form the comparative and superlative in this way: *luckier, luckiest.*)

Most two-syllable modifiers and all modifiers with three or more syllables use *more* or *most* to form the comparative and superlative degrees: *more beautiful, most beautiful; more quickly, most quickly.*

For negative comparisons, *less* and *least* are used before the positive form to form the comparative and superlative degrees: *less interesting, least interesting.*

A few adjectives and adverbs do not form the comparative and superlative degrees in the regular way. Since these irregular modifiers are used frequently, the forms should be memorized.

Positive	Comparative	Superlative
bad	worse	worst
far	farther or further	farthest or furthest
good, well	better	best
late	later	latest or last
little	less	least
many, much	more	most

Using Comparative and Superlative Forms of Adjectives and Adverbs

Decide whether the comparative or superlative form of the word in parentheses should be used in the sentence. Write the correct form of the adjective or adverb on the line.

1. All of these paintings are beautiful, but the still life by Cézanne appeals to me

   (much). _____

2. The photographs you took with this new camera are considerably (sharp) than

   the others. _____

3. Do you feel (well) today than you did last night? _____

4. The church of Hagia Sophia in Istanbul is one of the (spectacular) buildings

   in the world. _____

5. The report published by the Surgeon General is (specific) than the one printed

   in this pamphlet. _____

6. Between those two renditions of "The Star-Spangled Banner," hers was (bad). _____

Comparison of Adjectives and Adverbs

A. Using Comparative and Superlative Forms

Identify each boldfaced modifier as **C** for comparative or **S** for superlative. If the modifier is comparative, write the superlative form of the same modifier. If the modifier is superlative, write the comparative form of the same modifier.

1. Does the robin have **worse** sight than the eagle? _____

2. To me, the **most fascinating** animal we saw at the wildlife park was the mountain

   lion. _____

3. The **shortest** distance between two points is a straight line. _____

4. My home computer performs **more reliably** than the one in class. _____

5. Marina's costume for the party was original and Theo's was very funny, but John's

   was **best** of all. _____

B. Using Forms of Comparison

Underline the incorrect modifiers in the numbered sentences and write the correct modifiers below. Next to each correct modifier, write its degree: **P** for positive, **C** for comparative, and **S** for superlative.

Before the turn of the century, technological developments gave birth to the skyscraper, the building block of the modem metropolis. **(1)** Strongest than masonry or iron, steel skeletons allowed buildings to stretch to unbelievable heights. **(2)** In later years, skyscrapers with glistening glass exteriors became even most dominant on the urban landscape. **(3)** Some of the world's most spectacular skyscrapers, New York's Empire State Building and World Trade Center, and Chicago's Sears Tower, have at some point held the title of most tall building in the world. **(4)** Although some people find skyscrapers lease elegant than older, shorter buildings, skyscrapers can be integral to the city's identify. The words *New York City,* for instance, instantly conjure up images of a famous skyline. **(5)** Skyscraper proposals that are the more extraordinary are often opposed. **(6)** Although the best skyscrapers complement their older neighbors, the worse skyscrapers overwhelm and clash with their surroundings. Controversy over the height, design, and placement of skyscrapers continues to plague urban planners.

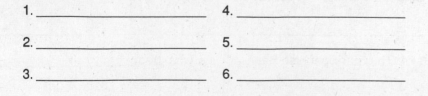

1. _____   4. _____

2. _____   5. _____

3. _____   6. _____

Using Comparisons Correctly

It is important to use comparisons correctly. Double comparisons, using *-er* and *more* together or *-est* and *most,* are incorrect.

> This tastes *more better.*   (incorrect)
> This tastes *better.*   (correct)

Illogical or confusing comparisons result if two unrelated items are compared or if something is compared with itself. To avoid illogical or confusing comparisons, remember:

1. The word *other* or the word *else* is required in the comparison of an individual member with the rest of the group: Pauline is a better violinist than any *other* violinist in the orchestra.
2. The word *than* or *as* is required after the first modifier in a compound comparison: Mr. Whitney is as tall *as,* if not taller than, Mr. Ranier.
3. Both parts of a comparison must be stated completely if there is any chance of a misunderstanding:

> I know Mary better than Ethel. (confusing)
> I know Mary better than I know Ethel. (clear)
> I know Mary better than Ethel does. (clear)

A. Identifying Correct Comparisons

Underline the word or words that correctly complete the comparison in each sentence.

1. Miguel practices more hours than (anyone, anyone else) on the team.

2. Kim enjoyed watching ballet more than (Michelle, Michelle did).

3. Ms. Peng is the (busiest, most busiest) of the three camp counselors.

4. Ellen is as (competent, competent as), if not more competent than, Wendy.

5. Tony wore the (funniest, most funniest) costume at the Halloween party.

B. Using Comparisons Correctly

Rewrite each sentence to correct the incorrect or illogical comparison.

1. Beth enjoys art more than Ann. _____

2. Dave has more endurance than any swimmer I know. _____

   _____

3. Of the two coins, the 1835 half-cent is most rarest. _____

   _____

4. Ms. Pratt commutes as far, if not farther than, Mr. Ita does. _____

   _____

5. Paul helped John more often than Mary. _____

   _____

Using Comparisons Correctly

A. Using Comparisons Correctly

Correct each sentence below. Underline any incorrect use of comparisons and write the correct form on the line. If you must add a word, write the phrase or clause that includes the necessary word on the line.

1. Do you like *Time* as much, or more than, *Newsweek?* _____

2. Justin is more taller than his younger brother, Nicholas. _____

3. I remember Alonzo more clearly than Gina. _____

4. The Mayor is better known than anyone in town. _____

5. The Clarks own the most oldest house in the country. _____

6. Which of the two candidates do you know more better? _____

7. Oba is more eloquent than any debater in the club. _____

8. What would be the most highest-paying job in the world? _____

B. Avoiding Incorrect Comparisons

Rewrite each numbered sentence to correct the double or illogical comparison.

With their versatility and wide dynamic range, stringed instruments such as the violin, viola, and cello are essential elements of an orchestra. **(1)** The violin is more widely played than any stringed instrument. **(2)** The violin, a popular solo instrument, is more smaller than the viola. **(3)** Despite its small size, the violin is as powerful if not more powerful than the cello. **(4)** Antonio Stradivari of seventeenth-century Italy once made the world's most finest violins. **(5)** Violin enthusiasts will tell you that the violin can produce a richer variety of sounds than any instrument.

1. _____

_____

2. _____

_____

3. _____

_____

4. _____

_____

5. _____

_____

Special Problems with Modifiers

Certain adjectives and adverbs have forms that can be confusing. *This* and *that* modify singular words: *this desk, that team. These* and *those* modify plural words: *those types, these uniforms.* The words *kind, sort,* and *type* require a singular modifier: *this kind, that type.*

Them is always a pronoun. *Those* may be either a pronoun or an adjective.

> Pick *them* pears when they are ripe. (incorrect)
> Pick *those* pears when they are ripe. (correct)

Bad is an adjective; *badly* is an adverb.

> *Bad* weather is forecast for tomorrow. (adjective)
> He fared *badly* in the tryouts. (adverb)

Good is an adjective; *well* can be either an adjective or an adverb. As an adjective, *well* means "in good health." As an adverb, it modifies an action verb.

> Melinda received a *good* report card. (adjective)
> Barry writes very *well.* (adverb)
> Louise feels *well* today. (adjective)

Do not use a double negative—two negative words used together where only one is necessary. Avoid the use of *hardly* or *barely* with a negative word.

> He doesn't like nothing. (incorrect)
> He doesn't like anything. (correct)

> There wasn't hardly any sunshine yesterday. (incorrect)
> There was hardly any sunshine yesterday. (correct)

Using Modifiers Correctly

Underline the correct word in parentheses in each sentence below.

1. The residents of Mackinac Island don't allow (any, no) cars on their streets.

2. (This, These) type of boot is good for walking through slush.

3. The coarse, scratchy fabric felt (bad, badly) against her skin.

4. I (could, couldn't) hardly see the stage without my glasses.

5. This brand of carpenter's glue works quite (good, well).

6. Responsible firms never authorize (that, those) kind of advertising.

7. Please put (those, them) socket wrenches in the garage.

8. Mrs. Heinz felt (well, good) about her research grant in biochemistry.

9. Water is one beverage that doesn't contain (any, no) calories.

10. Those (kind, kinds) of abrupt answers irritate me.

11. Don't wear (them, those) muddy shoes inside!

12. According to the doctor, Larry doesn't have (any, no) broken bones.

13. Don't feel (bad, badly) about your mistake; learn from it instead.

14. I (was, wasn't) barely able to hear the speaker.

15. The performance ended (good, well) after all.

Special Problems with Modifiers

A. Using Modifiers Correctly

Underline the correct word in parentheses in each sentence below.

1. John hasn't received (no, any) reply from the phone company about his bill.

2. The author writes (good, well), but I do not agree with her political views.

3. (This, These) type of problem seems to arise at the worst possible moment.

4. The new procedure for scheduling appointments is working (good, well).

5. The cheese you bought at the deli yesterday tastes (bad, badly).

6. Even though the weather forecast had been for a foot of snow, there (was, wasn't) hardly any snow on the ground by morning.

7. (Those, Them) instructions must be followed to the letter.

8. Susan felt (bad, badly) that she had missed the celebration.

9. Are (those, them) workers returning this afternoon to fix the elevator?

10. I have seen (this, these) sort of car before.

B. Correcting Special Problems with Modifiers

Rewrite each numbered sentence to correct the modifier problem.

John Muir, a nineteenth-century naturalist and wilderness advocate, fought for the conservation of nature through a national park system. **(1)** In Muir's day, there wasn't hardly anyone who agreed with him. **(2)** Few people felt badly about destroying forests that stood in the way of progress. **(3)** Muir, however, feared that if the exploitation continued unabated, there wouldn't be hardly any wilderness left. Muir fought to save California's Yosemite Valley and Arizona's Petrified Forest, among other places. **(4)** Thanks to Muir, we all can still enjoy them breathtaking wonders. **(5)** In his writings, Muir captured the beauty of the wilderness so good that he spawned an entire wilderness movement. The Sierra Club, founded by Muir, carries on a tradition of concern for the environment.

1. _____

2. _____
   _____

3. _____
   _____

4. _____

5. _____
   _____

Directions One or more of the underlined sections in the following sentences may contain errors of grammar, usage, punctuation, spelling, or capitalization. Write the letter of each incorrect section; then rewrite the item correctly. If there is no error in an item, write *E.* Write your answers on your own paper or on an answer sheet, as your teacher directs.

Example   To <u>us</u> sculptors, the physical strength of <u>Michelangelo's statue</u>
            A   **B**
            the *Pieta* is <u>his</u> <u>most unusual</u> quality. <u>No error</u>
                            C   **D**   **E**

Answer   C—its

1. Either Bob or Jim <u>is playing</u> <u>their</u> guitar at the festival; of the two musicians, both
                    A   **B**
    of <u>whom</u> have won all-city awards, Jim has the <u>best</u> chance of being selected.
        C   **D**
    <u>No error</u>
    E

2. The <u>most massive</u> of <u>them</u> icebergs <u>have been charted</u> by the U.S. Coast Guard,
            A   **B**   **C**
    <u>whose</u> tracking system is quite sophisticated. <u>No error</u>
    D   **E**

3. There <u>wasn't</u> hardly any decay on this ancient <u>Viking</u> ship excavated in Sweden in
            A   **B**
    the <u>1880's:</u> clay in the soil preserved the wood amazingly <u>good.</u> <u>No error</u>
        C   **D**   **E**

4. <u>Which of the two</u> tiny <u>European countries</u> is <u>smaller,</u> Liechtenstein or <u>Luxembourg?</u>
    A   **B**   **C**   **D**
    <u>No error</u>
    E

5. The word *palace* derives <u>it's</u> name from the Palatine Hill in Rome, where ancient
                    A   **B**
    <u>Romans</u> built <u>there</u> fashionable houses. <u>No error</u>
    C   **D**   **E**

6. The <u>larger</u> of the two <u>dioramas, which</u> shows a <u>medieval manor,</u> was created by
        A   **B**   **C**
    the three of us—Deirdre, Wesley, and <u>I.</u> <u>No error</u>
                                        D **E**

7. Although the detective <u>who</u> we hired identified a <u>suspect,</u> she <u>didn't know</u>
                     A   **B**   **C**

   the <u>most effective</u> way to find the evidence. <u>No error</u>
          D   **E**

8. Although everyone in our class <u>think that</u> the crossword puzzle is a
                                  A

   <u>recent invention,</u> it was <u>actually invented</u> in 1913 by an <u>American</u> named Arthur
      B   **C**   **D**

   Winn. <u>No error</u>
         E

9. For <u>myself</u>, the rehearsal proceeded <u>smoothly</u> because I had practiced
          A   **B**

   <u>more hours</u> than <u>anyone</u> in the cast. <u>No error</u>
      C   **D**   **E**

10. The <u>saleswoman and us</u> think that, of <u>those</u> two jackets, the tweed one with the
            A   **B**

   narrow lapels <u>fit</u> <u>best</u>. <u>No error</u>
               C **D**   **E**

11. Jayne Torvill is one of the <u>most gracefullest</u> performers in the sport of ice
                             A

   <u>dancing; her</u> and her <u>partner, Christopher Dean,</u> won an <u>Olympic</u> Gold Medal in
      B   **C**   **D**

   1984. <u>No error</u>
         E

12. The birds started <u>their singing</u> <u>earlier</u> today than they did yesterday, waking
                  A   **B**

   <u>us poor sleepers</u> from <u>our well-deserved</u> rest. <u>No error</u>
      C   **D**   **E**

13. Each of the marathon runners <u>accepted</u> <u>their drink</u> from <u>whoever</u> <u>was standing</u> on
                             A   **B**   **C**   **D**

   the curb. <u>No error</u>
             E

14. <u>The biologist James D. Watson</u> helped to discover the structure of
                 A

   <u>DNA, as a result,</u> the <u>Nobel Prize</u> in Medicine was awarded to
      B   **C**

   <u>he and Francis Crick</u> in 1962. <u>No error</u>
      D   **E**

15. The <u>worst</u> score of the day was <u>her's,</u> but the winners of the contest, <u>him and me,</u>
      A   **B**   **C**

   scored only ten points <u>higher than she</u>. <u>No error</u>
                    D   **E**

Directions Read the passage and chose the word or group of words that belongs in each numbered space. Write the letter of the correct answer on your own paper or on an answer sheet, as your teacher directs.

Example   Some cities in the Middle East obtain ___(1)___ drinking water from the sea. However, purifying water in desalination plants is ___(2)___ than using other sources of drinking water.

1. A. it's
   B. its
   C. their
   D. they're

2. A. expensiver
   B. more expensive
   C. expensivest
   D. most expensive

Answers   1—C   2—B

No disease of the Middle Ages was ___(16)___ than the bubonic plague, or Black Death. This plague, which killed one-third of Europe's population in the 1300's, ___(17)___ by fleas that lived on ___(18)___ doctors at the time knew no more than ___(19)___ about germs. The typical community, therefore, blamed ___(20)___ wished for the disease—cats, strangers, or even witches and supernatural forces. Ship rats carried the plague from port to port. As the disease spread ___(21)___ inland, the number of deaths soared.

16. A. deadlier
    B. more deadlier
    C. most deadly
    D. deadliest

17. A. was spread
    B. were spread
    C. is spread
    D. are spread

18. A. rats: unfortunately
    B. rats, unfortunately
    C. rats; unfortunately,
    D. rats; Unfortunately

19. A. anybody
    B. nobody
    C. anybody else
    D. nobody else

20. A. whoever it
    B. whomever it
    C. whoever they
    D. whomever they

21. A. farther
    B. further
    C. more farther
    D. more further

The nursery rhyme ___(22)___ describes the Black Death. A rosy-colored ring on the skin was the first symptom of the disease. Some people carried posies, or flowers, in their pockets to protect ___(23)___. Of course, ___(24)___ kind of protection was useless. Instead of burial, bodies were often burned to ashes since this method of disposal took care of the problem ___(25)___ than any other. Some people feared that everyone would fall down dead from the disease.

22. A. Ring Around the Rosie
    B. , Ring Around the Rosie,
    C. , "Ring Around the Rosie,"
    D. "Ring Around the Rosie"

23. A. theirself
    B. theirselves
    C. them
    D. themselves

24. A. this
    B. them
    C. these
    D. those

25. A. more rapid
    B. rapider
    C. more rapidly
    D. most rapidly

Personal Titles, Nationalities, and Religions

A **proper noun** is the name of a specific person, place, thing, or idea. A **proper adjective** is formed from a proper noun. Capitalize both proper nouns and proper adjectives.

> Did *Napoleon Bonaparte* reach *St. Petersburg* in the *War of 1812?*
> Are *Maltese* cats as highly valued as *Manx* or *Persian* cats?

Capitalize people's names, initials, titles, and abbreviations for titles. Also capitalize *Jr.* and *Sr.* after names. Capitalize a title used without a person's name if it refers to a head of state or to someone in an important position.

> When *Cassie* called herself *Cassandra G. Henry, Jr., Dr. Halpin* smiled.
> *Queen Elizabeth's* first son bears the title *Prince of Wales.*
> The *Prime Minister* greeted the *President* and four governors.

Capitalize titles indicating family relationships when the titles are used as names or parts of names. Do not capitalize titles used as common nouns.

> I have five uncles, but my favorite is *Uncle Jim.*

Capitalize the names of races, languages, nationalities, and religions, and any adjectives formed from these names.

> The early *Irish* monks decorated their *Latin* texts with a combination of *Christian* symbols and elaborate *Celtic* designs.

Capitalize all words referring to God, the Holy Family, and religious scriptures, as well as any personal pronouns referring to God. Always capitalize the pronoun *I*.

> The prayer began, "O, *Allah,* give us *Thy* blessings."
> Below the portrait of the *Madonna* was a quote, *I* think, from *Luke.*

In hyphenated compound words, capitalize the parts that are capitalized when they stand alone.

> "I'm not *anti-American* or *pro-Communist.* I'm neutral," the diplomat said.

Capitalizing Correctly

Underline each word that should be capitalized.

1. The hittites were the earliest known inhabitants of turkey.

2. Which governor of california gave his name to a university?

3. The vedas are the ancient scriptures of the indian religion known as hinduism.

4. The koran is the sacred book of the muslims.

5. Ms. martin is studying for a degree in african art.

6. Johnny appleseed planted many trees in frontier areas of ohio and indiana.

7. My aunt collects pre-civil war antiques.

8. Is that the scholar who is an expert in african-american history?

9. "The lord is my shepherd" is the first line of psalm 23.

10. The lecture by professor mara covered ashanti myths.

11. The defendant's lawyer, p. david powers, jr., stood before judge marshall.

12. The first line of the gospel of john echoes the first line of genesis.

Personal Titles, Nationalities, Religions

A. Capitalizing Correctly
Underline each word that should be capitalized.

1. The dutch inventor hans lippershey built a telescope in 1608.

2. Although a devout roman catholic, joan of arc was burned as a witch.

3. One girl who claimed to have seen the virgin mary became a saint.

4. Is soy sauce used in both chinese and japanese cooking?

5. As a result of the invasion by the chinese, the head of lamaism—the dalai lama—was forced to flee tibet in 1959.

6. The keynote speaker was the chief justice of the united states supreme court.

7. Writing about cooking can be amusing, as m. f. k. fisher's books prove so well.

8. When did gen. eisenhower become a five-star general?

9. My aunt hopes to interview ex-representative mink of hawaii.

10. Did you know that a native of tennessee named sequoya not only created an 86-character alphabet for the cherokee language, but also opened america's first cherokee-engligh newspaper?

B. Using Correct Capitalization
Write capital letters above the lower-case letters as needed.

(1) the story of helen keller begins with how a child at the age of eighteen months was struck deaf, blind, and mute by scarlet fever. (2) Against overwhelming odds she overcame these handicaps. (3) She had the help of her teacher, annie sullivan, and the inventor alexander graham bell.

(4) Annie sullivan came to the keller household when helen was seven. (5) Annie became helen's lifelong teacher and friend. (6) How miss sullivan turned the child into a responsible human being and awakened her marvelous mind is familiar to millions, most notably through william gibson's play and film *The Miracle Worker*.

(7) Helen keller had a writing career for fifty years. (8) Her autobiography is available in more than fifty languages, including pushtu and tagalog. (9) She was given many awards, including the brazilian Order of the Southern Cross and the lebanese Gold Medal of Merit. (10) She met every president from grover cleveland to john f. kennedy and even met prime minster nehru of india.

In a geographical name, capitalize the first letter of each word but not articles and prepositions (*the Al-Can Highway, the Cape of Good Hope*). Capitalize the word modified by a proper adjective only if the noun and adjective together form a geographical name (*Mexico City, the English Channel* but *Mexican food, an English city.*)

Capitalize the names of sections of the country or the world and any adjectives that come from these sections. Do not capitalize compass directions or adjectives indicating mere direction or general location (*Far East, the Deep South, South Korea, the Orient, a Western drawl* but *drive east, the southern coastline, traveling northward*).

Capitalize the names of planets and other objects in the universe, except *sun* and *moon* (*Venus, the North Star, the Milky Way, Jupiter's Red Spot, the sun's rays*). However, capitalize the word *earth* only when it is used in conjunction with the names of the other planets (*an Earth-to-Mars signal* but *to farm the earth*).

Capitalize the names of specific monuments, bridges, buildings, ships, trains, airplanes, automobiles, and spacecraft (*Eiffel Tower, Verrazano Bridge, White House, U.S.S. Missouri, Orient Express, Air Force One, Challenger*).

Understanding Capitalization

Underline the words that should be capitalized in the following sentences.

1. From above, the great barrier reef looks like a watery great wall of china.

2. This buffer between australia's northeastern coast and the coral sea is surely one of the earth's natural jewels; it adorns 12,500 miles of the queensland coastline.

3. The continent beyond is divided into three official regions: the eastern highlands, the central lowlands, and the western plateau.

4. Cities hug the rim, circling from northernmost darwin west, south, and finally eastward up to sydney (named after the english statesman viscount sydney).

5. Explorers from holland wrote off this land as useless, but one englishman did not.

6. The land Capt. James Cook "discovered" when he sailed the *endeavor* into botany bay in 1770 had already been inhabited for 50,000 years by natives.

7. The discovery was a bonus, for scientists on board had already fulfilled their goal, having stopped in tahiti to watch venus pass between earth and the sun.

8. The captain proceeded to name the bay for its rich plant life, to call the area new south wales, and to claim it for King George III and great britain.

9. Eight years later, eleven ships—now called the first fleet—sailed into the bay.

10. Finding it too swampy, they moved northward to sydney cove (now port jackson).

11. What started as a british convict colony became the nation's busiest port and a center of american-european trade and asian investment.

12. Its frontier spirit is reminiscent of our own west a century ago.

13. Bold modern buildings such as the m.l.c. centre signal that brash optimism.

14. Since 1973 the Sydney opera house, known for its saillike roof, has attracted visitors from anchorage to zimbabwe.

15. Cook never found the northwest passage; instead, he opened up a new world.

Geographical Names, Structures, and Vehicles

A. Capitalizing Correctly

Underline the letters that should be capitals in the following sentences. If a sentence is already correct, write **Correct** in the blank.

1. The sun rises in the east and sets in the west. _____

2. The st. lawrence seaway links the atlantic to the great lakes. _____

3. We drove on u.s. highway 94 from detroit to chicago. _____

4. The earth is in the galaxy called the milky way. _____

5. The *petrol prince* is a supertanker that carries millions of barrels of oil. _____

6. Rocky mountain national park is in colorado. _____

B. Using Correct Capitalization

Write capital letters above the lower-case letters where needed.

(1) The islands of bimini lie fifty miles east of miami, in a tourist haven warmed by the gulf stream. (2) They are part of the island chain known as the bahamas.

(3) Between the islands of north and south bimini is a shallow lagoon that abounds with lemon sharks.

(4) The *bahamas prince,* an airboat, carries photographers and researchers to the lagoon from the small harbor of alicetown. (5) Sharkman Sam, the bahamian guide who operates the craft, knows more about the lemon shark than perhaps does anyone else on earth. (6) Tourists from cruisers such as the *queen elizabeth 2* flock to Sam's boat to investigate the shark's lagoon habitat.

(7) Scientists who have studied these sharks off the islands of bimini have found them to be quite gentle. (8) Eating only about every four days, the sharks certainly do not fit the stereotypic "eating machines" popularized in books and films. (9) Furthermore, they are relatively shy, staying in the lagoon for the first five years of their lives. (10) When mature, they leave to wander in small groups in various parts of the atlantic ocean. (11) The sharks may swim as far north as new jersey and as far south as brazil, but they return each may to the lagoon.

Organizations, Events, and Other Subjects

Capitalize all words in the names of organizations and institutions except articles, conjunctions, and prepositions (*the House of Representatives*). Also capitalize abbreviations for such names (*Trans World Airlines, TWA*). Do not capitalize words such as *school* and *church* when they are not parts of names.

> The *Peace Corps* was founded during the Kennedy administration.
> The *University of Southern California* is affectionately known as *USC*.

Capitalize the names of historical events, documents, and periods of time; the names of months, days, and holidays, but not the names of seasons (*Memorial Day* but *the first day of summer*); and the abbreviations B.C., A.D., A.M., and P.M.

> The *Diaspora* began in the *1200's* B.C., when Moses led the *Exodus*; the *Passover* festival commemorates this escape.
> *Magna Carta* was signed in *June* of A.D. *1215* at Runnymede.

Capitalize the names of awards and special events. Also capitalize the names of specific school courses, but not the general names of school subjects.

> Who won the first *World Series* and the first *Cy Young Award*?
> Since Julie is strong in *mathematics*, she will take *Calculus I* next year.

Capitalize the brand names of products but not common nouns that follow brand names (*Mountain Springs* sparkling water).

Using Correct Capitalization

Underline the words that should be capitalized in the following sentences.

1. The university of iowa offers a good education and an exciting athletic program.

2. Do you know the name of our delegate to the united nations?

3. The bill of rights is the name of the first ten amendments to the constitution.

4. On july 1 Canadians celebrate canada day, which until 1982 was called dominion day.

5. The conqueror alexander the great was born in 356 b.c.

6. The first oscar was bestowed at an academy awards ceremony in 1928.

7. We feed our parakeets bird banquet birdseed and no other brand.

8. The bureau of labor statistics publishes facts about u.s. workers.

9. The reformation was a religious movement of the sixteenth century.

10. On election day, the first tuesday after the first monday in november, the polls are open from 7:00 a.m. to 7:00 p.m.

11. The tournament of roses parade precedes the football game at the rose bowl.

12. Coach Franklin teaches three health courses and drivers' education I and II.

13. The marshall plan helped european nations recover after world war II.

14. The national collegiate athletic association set standards and rules for college sports.

15. Do you believe that groundhog day marks the official beginning of spring?

Organizations, Events, and Other Subjects

A. Capitalizing Correctly

Write capital letters above the lower-case letters where they are needed in the following paragraphs.

(1) On thursday, november 21, 1963, President John F. Kennedy and his wife, Jacqueline, traveled on *Air Force One* to San Antonio, Texas. (2) There, Kennedy gave a speech at the brooks medical center.

(3) The next morning their plane took them from Fort Worth to Love Field, in Dallas, landing at 11:39 a.m. (4) By noon, they were in a motorcade headed for the dallas trade mart, where Kennedy was to give a speech. (5) The cars traveled slowly, and members of the secret service walked alongside the President's open limousine. (6) As the cars approached the texas school book depository building at 12:30 p.m., the first of three shots rang out.

(7) President John F. Kennedy died on friday, november 22, 1963, at 1:00 p.m. (8) This was the first of three political killings that would stun the nation. (9) Soon Martin Luther King, Jr., civil rights leader and winner of a nobel peace prize, would also be assassinated. (10) In june 1968, Robert Kennedy, on tour for the democratic nomination for President, would be gunned down. (11) The warren commission was formed to investigate John F. Kennedy's death, but controversy still surrounds all three events.

B. Using Correct Capitalization

Suppose that you are asked to introduce a dignitary at your school assembly. Write a short introduction for that person. Use imaginary people, places, and things to include proper nouns and proper adjectives. Draft your introduction on a separate sheet of paper and write the final version on the lines below.

_____

_____

_____

_____

_____

_____

Capitalize the first word of every sentence, the first word of every line of poetry, and the first word of a direct quotation. In a divided quotation, do not capitalize the first word of the second part unless it starts a new sentence.

> "Peace," the ambassador said, "can only be achieved through cooperation."
> "There's no time like the present," she said. "Let's begin."

In a letter, capitalize the greeting, the person's title and name, and words such as *Sir* and *Madam*. Capitalize only the first word in the complimentary close.

> Dear Ms. Evans,
>
> I accept with pleasure your invitation to attend the awards ceremony for volunteers at the Thompson Clinic. I look forward to seeing you there.
>
> Yours sincerely,
> James Trumball-Smith

Capitalize the first word of each item in an outline and letters that introduce major subsections.

> I. Nineteenth-century immigration
>   A. Reasons for immigration
>   1. Among Europeans
>   a. The Irish potato famine
>   b. Upheavals from war
>   2. Among Asians

Capitalize the first, last, and all other important words in titles. Do not capitalize conjunctions, articles, or prepositions with fewer than five letters.

> My paper is called "The Importance of Rachel Carson's *Silent Spring*."

Capitalizing First Words and Titles

Underline the letters that should be capitals in the following items.

1. "double, double, toil and trouble;

    fire burn, and cauldron bubble." *William Shakespeare*

2. todd said, "i wonder if Bigfoot really exists."

3. "there's a big shadow in the field," Al said. "it's from that hot-air balloon."

4. dear mr. chung: enclosed are your tickets for the play. yours truly, Mrs. Haas

5. I. vertebrates

      a. reptiles

        1. snakes

6. "half the truth," Benjamin Franklin said, "is often a gentle lie."

7. we studied *the iliad* by homer, a Greek who lived about 750 B.C.

8. in American history class we studied the declaration of independence.

9. i have borrowed my brother's copy of *two years before the mast*.

10. wallace Steven's poem "anecdote of the jar" is a modern American response to

    Keats's "ode on a grecian urn."

First Words and Titles

A. Capitalizing First Words and Titles

Underline the letters that should be capitals in the following sentences.

1. The *american chemical journal* was first published in 1879.
2. Frank Loesser's musical *guys and dolls* was based on Damon runyan's collection of the same name, especially the short story "the idyll of miss sarah brown."
3. Recently, *time* magazine had an article titled "DNA: secret of life."
4. Willie Loman is the main character in Arthur Miller's play *death of a salesman.*
5. The TV show *60 minutes* has been on for more than a decade.

B. Using Correct Capitalization

Write capital letters above the lower-case letters where needed below.

(1) For over a century, controversy has raged about the authorship of the poems and plays, including *hamlet*, credited to William Shakespeare. **(2)** some people think the philosopher Francis Bacon wrote the plays. **(3)** others think the Earl of Oxford did. **(4)** "no doubt," says Shakespearean actor Ian McKellen, "somewhere there's a viewer of the TV series *masterpiece theatre* who thinks the host of that show wrote the plays." **(5)** charlton Ogburn, author of the book *mysterious william Shakespeare,* argues that the Earl of Oxford wrote the plays. **(6)** ogburn says that Shakespeare was too unlearned and common to have written most of them. **(7)** For example, the author of *richard III* and *hamlet* had a vocabulary of more than twenty thousand words, including over one hundred musical terms and the names of two hundred plants. **(8)** since the Earl of Oxford was educated, talented as a poet, and well traveled (and therefore acquainted with the foreign settings of many of the plays), Ogburn believes that he could indeed be the author. **(9)** places and events in Oxford's life are similar to those in *othello, hamlet, love's labour's lost,* and other plays. **(10)** shakespeare, on the other hand, may never have left southeast England. **(11)** despite research by historians for over three hundred years, the facts of Shakespeare's life will fit on an index card. **(12)** perhaps this lack of background points to Shakespeare as a pen name for another writer. **(13)** to find our how little we really know, read the article "some ado about who was, or was not, Shakespeare."

End Marks

Use a **period** at the end of all declarative sentences, most imperative sentences, and indirect questions.

The capital of Cyprus is Nicosia. (declarative)
Close the door. (imperative)
The man asked where the station was. (indirect question)

Also use a period at the end of an abbreviation or an initial (*M. F. K. Fisher*), after each number or letter in an outline or list, between dollars and cents (*$20.89*), and to indicate a decimal.

For abbreviations of metric measurements, acronyms, and abbreviations that are pronounced letter by letter, periods are optional: *kg, NASA, CIA.*

Use a **question mark** at the end of an interrogative sentence or after a question that is not a complete sentence.

What time is it?   How many?   Why?   Really?

Use an **exclamation point** at the end of an exclamatory sentence or after a strong interjection.

That's impossible!   Help!   Wow!   Yes!

Using End Marks Correctly

Add periods, exclamation points, and question marks where needed in each of the following sentences.

1. Are T S Eliot and W H Auden two great modern poets

2. Texas governor John B Connally, Jr, was riding with John F Kennedy the day

   Kennedy was assassinated

3. The first ten amendments to the US Constitution make up the Bill of Rights

4. Read the section on Polish astronomer Nicolaus Copernicus for tomorrow

5. The musical *Fiddler on the Roof* is based on short stories by Sholom Aleichem

6. Wow That was too close for comfort

7. The US Department of Housing and Urban Development is referred to as HUD

8. Reporters asked about the role of the new director of the CIA

9. I   Fruits
       A Berries
           1   Raspberries
           2   Blackberries

10. How much Are you really asking $4575 for a hammer worth only $1250

11. It's fantastic that the snowstorm bypassed us

12. The police officer asked how the accident happened

13. T E Lawrence is perhaps best known as Lawrence of Arabia

14. Did the Great Depression begin in 1928 or 1929

15. The musical *My Fair Lady* was based on G B Shaw's play *Pygmalion*

End Marks

A. Using End Marks

Add periods, exclamation points, and question marks where needed in the following sentences. Draw a line through any period, exclamation point, or question mark that does not belong, and add the correct mark.

1. The Kremlin is the seat of government in the USSR
2. Tuberculosis was the leading cause of US deaths in 1900
3. Hooray We've won the debate tournament
4. Have you ever studied ballet or modern dance
5. How wonderful it is to meet you.
6. The OMB is the Office of Management and Budget of the US government
7. Ms B B Clough of Detroit, Michigan, won the grand prize
8. At 9:15 AM the satellite was launched
9. Imagine He'll be one year old next Thursday
10. How clever you are to have figured out that maze
11. Would you like to go to dinner some evening next week
12. I wonder what's on television tonight
13. The cabin attendant asked if I wanted a pillow and blanket?
14. The time. It's exactly 1:36 PM
15. Wait Don't you see that car coming!
16. Whew. What a long day it's been

B. Using End Marks in Paragraphs

Add periods, exclamation points, and question marks where they are needed in the following paragraphs.

Achoo Have you ever wondered where sneezes come from Sneezing is a sudden and violent rush of air through the nose and mouth A person has no control over it The body creates a sneeze to get rid of irritating objects in the nose You might ask why bright sunlight can also cause sneezing This is because the eye nerves are closely connected with nerve endings in the nose

The way you sneeze is probably hereditary, according to Dr Murray A Gordon, Jr, of Oklahoma's Grant Hospital A common inherited pattern is the "double sneeze," in which two sneezes occur just a few seconds apart Babies only a few weeks old have been known to sneeze in family patterns Although you can watch others sneeze, you can't watch yourself Have you ever noticed that it's impossible to sneeze with your eyes open if you want to know how you look when you sneeze, watch your parents

Use of the Comma (I)

Use a comma after every item in a series except the last one.

For breakfast we had eggs, bacon, and toast. (series of words)
We looked for the bracelet under the bed, behind the cushions, and in the dresser drawers. (series of phrases)
The counselor asked Ellen what her career goal was, what college she hoped to attend, and what her major would be. (series of clauses)

Use commas after *first, second,* and so on, when these words introduce a series.

Fans arrived in three ways: first, by car; second, by train; third, on foot.

Use commas between coordinate adjectives that modify the same noun. Coordinate adjectives are of equal rank and can be revered in order without changing the meaning of the sentence.

The persistent, creative artist painted a picture before daybreak.

Using Commas Correctly

Insert commas where they are needed in the following sentences. Cross out any comma that is not necessary.

1. We toured the gardens in the following sequence: first the herb garden; second the lily pond; third the camellia garden; fourth the rose garden.

2. The oil in the jojoba plant is used in food preparation in lubricants for automobiles and in cosmetics.

3. Prickly pear cacti have flattened padlike stems.

4. The aloe plant bears flowers that are red yellow and orange.

5. While walking through the garden, we were awed by the size of the eucalyptus trees the beauty of the water lilies and the agelessness of the yuccas.

6. We enjoyed the different names of the cacti: the elephant's foot the living rock cacti the pincushion cacti and the houseleek.

7. The white flowers of the epiphytic cacti the yellow of the golden barrel cacti and the flowering stalk of the yucca were striking in their beauty.

8. We decided that upon our return home we would begin an herb garden that we would plant annuals and that we would tend these gardens every day.

9. Camellias have shiny dark leaves with heavy waxy petals.

10. The blossoms of the camellia may be red white pink or spotted with color.

11. The three main classes of cultivated roses are the following: first the old rose; second the perpetual rose; third the everblooming hybrid.

12. The fragrant lovely, rose is one of the most beautiful of all flowers.

13. The roses we saw were red yellow various shades of pink and white.

14. Sweetbriar roses are tall graceful roses with fragrant, leaves.

15. We decided that these were the things we liked best in the gardens: first the sweetbriar roses; second the golden barrel cactus; third the red camellias.

Use of the Comma (I)

Form B

A. Using Commas
Insert commas where they are needed in the following sentences. Cross out any comma that is not necessary.

1. Cary Grant Humphrey Bogart and Robert De Niro are three of my favorite actors.
2. The talented charismatic actress received a standing ovation.
3. When they perform in a play actors must be attentive to lighting signals from other actors and the use of stage props.
4. The director explains what the actors should say how they should say it and, where they should stand while speaking.
5. Every actor actress and director hopes for success, on Broadway in Hollywood or on TV.

B. Using Commas in Paragraphs
Add commas where they are needed in the following paragraphs.

Many novels have been made into movies. The film *The Grapes of Wrath* was based on the novel by John Steinbeck. The story centers on an Oklahoma family named the Joads. They lose their home by bank foreclosure in the 1930's pack up their meager belongings and migrate to California to start a new life. The film starred Henry Fonda Jane Darwell and John Carradine. The talented creative actors worked together to convey a feeling of compassion for the poor.

Oliver! was a musical based on Charles Dickens's novel *Oliver Twist*. The fantastic choreography lively music and spectacular setting made this movie a memorable one. The songs "Consider Yourself" and "Food, Glorious Food" remain popular.

Of course, no one can forget the movie *Bambi* when discussing novels that were made into movies. This heartwarming engaging story is an animated film. It was based on the novel of the same title written by Felix Salten. The character of Thumper the wonderful animation and the bittersweet story have made this a memorable film for generation after generation of moviegoers.

Shakespearean plays have also been presented in film. *Henry V* is one of Shakespeare's historical plays that was made into a movie and nominated for an Academy Award. Laurence Olivier Robert Newton Leslie Banks and Esmond Knight were among the impressive cast. The movie was outstanding in many respects: first the acting was exceptional; second the color photography was spectacular; third the historical representation of the Globe Theater of the early 1600's gave the audience a sense of what it would have been like to view this play in Shakespeare's day.

144 *Handbook 39   End Marks and Commas*

Use of the Comma (II)

Use a comma after introductory words, mild interjections, or adverbs at the beginning of a sentence.

> By the way, may I call you tomorrow?
> Oh, I didn't think you were here.
> Nevertheless, the play will open as scheduled.

Use a comma after a series of prepositional phrases, after verbal phrases, and after adverbial clauses at the beginning of sentences. Use a comma after words or phrases that have been transposed; that is, moved to the beginning of a sentence from their normal position.

> In the old green barn behind the house, our cat Trixie sat quietly.
> To apply for a scholarship, complete the attached forms.
> When Peter entered the room, the guests yelled "Surprise!"
> If necessary, borrow the money from your sister.

Use commas to set off nonessential appositives.

> Mswati III, the King of Swaziland, was only eighteen on his coronation day.

Do not use commas with essential appositives.

> The movie *Great Expectations* won an Academy Award.

Use commas to set off words of direct address and parenthetical expressions.

> Tonya, be sure to include a self-addressed envelope.
> You are, I believe, one of the five applicants being considered for the job.

Using Commas Correctly

Insert commas where they are needed in the following sentences.

1. These ties Dad are too old-fashioned.

2. Toronto the capital of Ontario is Canada's second-largest city.

3. In fact *Millions of Cats* is one of my favorite books.

4. Consequently many students apply.

5. At the beginning of the season we knew we could win.

6. Wearing black robes and white wigs the British judges entered the courtroom.

7. Well I've done as much as I can for one day.

8. To play the piano well a person needs nimble fingers.

9. After weeks of deliberation in the courtroom the jury found him guilty.

10. Atop a pear tree at the end of the road a crow perched.

11. If necessary Max will cancel tonight's meeting.

12. The French Quarter also known as Vieux Carré is a famous area of New Orleans.

13. It is important to take lessons before you begin Roger.

14. By the way we will be finished with the term paper before the weekend.

15. Obviously you will need to have a physical examination.

Use of the Comma (II)

A. Using Commas

Insert commas where they are needed in the following sentences. If a sentence is correct, write **Correct** in the blank.

1. Charles Spencer Chaplin a famous slapstick comedian spent most of his life in the entertainment business. _____

2. Even when he was a toddler Chaplin liked to perform vaudeville routines. He was quite an amazing talent. _____

3. His first professional act was performed I believe by the time he was nine years old. _____

4. Rena have you read the biography of Charlie Chaplin—the one about his career as a famous silent film comedian? _____

5. Yes I enjoyed it tremendously. _____

6. The movie *City Lights* is my favorite Chaplin film. _____

B. Using Commas in Paragraphs

Add commas where they are needed in the following paragraphs.

Although Charlie Chaplin's films are varied in their content they are always entertaining to watch. Chaplin's first movie *Making a Living* met with mixed reviews. Some felt the movie was funny. However others felt that in a high hat and frock coat Charlie looked too much like the villain audiences had seen in many previous stage shows.

In a later film entitled *Work* Charlie is an assistant to Izzy A. Wake. Izzy a painter and a paper hanger finds himself in a variety of slapstick situations. Once again the critical reviews were mixed. Some reviewers felt Chaplin showed genius in presenting the slapstick; others it seems felt that the film was poorly put together and had little merit.

For many people of all ages a favorite Chaplin film is *Modern Times*. In this movie Charlie a factory worker gets caught in a huge machine while he is oiling it. Charlie you can be sure passes through the machine safely. Consequently he is chosen to test a new machine. The new machine is supposed to help feed lunch to a worker in a shorter period of time. The machine of course does not work. In fact nothing works except the mouth wiper. Unlike some of Charlie's other films *Modern Times* received excellent critical reviews. Critics who wrote for such newspapers as the *New York Post* and *The New York Times* thought that once more Chaplin showed his genius.

Commas: Quotations and Clauses

Use commas to set off the explanatory words of a direct quotation. When the explanatory words follow the quotation, a comma belongs at the end of the quotation inside the quotation marks.

> Jean exclaimed, "What a beautiful sunset!"
> "The washing machine is out of order," reported Mike.

In a divided quotation, use a comma within the quotation marks after the first part of the quotation and after the explanatory words.

> "Let's play tennis," suggested Mark, "and then we can go biking."

Use a comma before the conjunction that joins the two main clauses of a compound sentence. Also use commas to set off nonessential clauses and to set off nonessential participial phrases.

> Ginny enjoys reading biographies of artists and composers, but Gerry likes historical novels set in eighteenth-century France.
> Ella's dance teacher, who was formerly a ballerina, is very demanding.
> The salad, consisting of organically grown greens, was delicious.

Using Commas

Insert commas where they are needed in the following sentences.

1. The tornado ripped through the city yet no one was injured.

2. The abacus which has beads arranged in columns is a type of calculator.

3. I gave Nicole the money and she gave me the ticket for the performance.

4. "Today" said Police Chief White "is a great day for the police academy."

5. The Battle of Gettysburg which was fought from July 1 through July 3, 1863 marked a turning point in the Civil War.

6. Gothic architecture which originated in France during the late Middle Ages features ribbed vaults, pointed arches, and flying buttresses.

7. Lou who is not a good sailor was apprehensive sailing around Cape Hatteras.

8. "Knowledge may give weight but accomplishments give luster" wrote Lord Chesterfield "and many more people see than weigh."

9. Roberta who is a well-organized person proved an able administrator.

10. Pressed for time Allan took the shortest route to the campsite.

11. Steve wondered "What will I be doing ten years from now?"

12. Robert Louis Stevenson wrote "No man is useless while he has a friend."

13. Tom has always wanted to learn how to sail that boat but he will need to learn how to swim first.

14. "I'll never finish this in time to make the deadline" the reporter complained "unless you help me."

15. My dog terrified by the thunder jumped into bed with me.

Commas: Quotations and Clauses

A. Using Commas
In the following sentences, insert commas where they are needed.

1. "The river" said the scientist "will overflow its banks by tomorrow morning."
2. Mozart learned to play the harpsichord at age four and he completed his first symphony at age eight.
3. Cleveland which is located on Lake Erie is where I grew up.
4. Vincent van Gogh who suffered from epilepsy produced an enormous number of paintings despite his disability.
5. "The Knights of Labor was an early American union" Tom explained to the class.
6. The snow-capped Rockies rising high above the Plains presented a formidable barrier to the wagon trains heading for California.
7. Corazón Aquino who is the President of the Philippines lived for many years in the United States.
8. Scientists have made many great discoveries yet they have not found a cure for the common cold.
9. The paleontologist exclaimed "These bones are over 200 million years old!"
10. Petunia an oil well on the lawn of Oklahoma's capitol went dry in January 1986.

B. Using Commas in Paragraphs
The following passage tests many of the comma rules you have studied. Add commas where they are needed.

You may enjoy listening to music through headphones but you may be risking hearing damage. Hearing specialists recognizing the potential for injury urge listeners to turn down the volume.

"Generally, portable headphones turned up to more than half the total volume capacity are loud enough to cause both temporary and permanent hearing loss" says Richard O'Connors. O'Connors who is a professor at Utah State University School of Medicine in Logan recently studied eighteen different brands of portable headphones. He found that some were powerful enough to inflict damage at even half their full volume which can reach an ear-splitting 115 decibels. This damage includes loss of hearing which can occur if exposures exceed ninety decibels for long periods of time.

If someone can hear your music from three feet away when you're wearing earphones you have the volume up too high. "People do need to be cautioned" notes Dr. O'Connors "but with moderate use of no more than two hours daily headphones are safe for most people."

Commas: Other Uses

In dates, use a comma between the day of the month and the year: *May 12, 1952.* When only the month and year are given, no comma is necessary: *May 1952.*

Use a comma between the name of a city or town and the name of its state or country, after the salutation of a friendly letter, and after the complimentary closing of a friendly letter or a business letter.

> Oslo, Norway   Dear Penny,   Sincerely yours,

Use a comma after the year and after the last item in an address when a date or an address comes in the middle of a sentence.

> July 13, 1975, is the date of my birth.
> Write to me at 6 Wyn Street, Provo, Utah 84601, after May 1.

Use a comma to separate words or phrases that might mistakenly be joined when read and to indicate the words left out of parallel word groups.

> In brief, speeches should attract the attention of the audience.
> Franklin Roosevelt was elected President four times; Ronald Reagan, twice.

Use commas when a name is followed by one or more titles and after a business abbreviation if it is part of a sentence.

> David Case, Ph.D., is joining L. G. Computers, Inc., in his home town.

In numbers of more than three digits, use a comma after every third digit from the right, except in ZIP codes, phone numbers, years, and house numbers.

> population of 210,000   Naugatuck, CT 06770   2051 Main Street

Using Commas

Insert commas where they belong in the following items.

1. John Adams and Thomas Jefferson both died on July 4 1826 in their home states.

2. In Dover Delaware a major industry is the manufacture of latex products.

3. Dear Joe Enclosed is the catalog I was telling you about. Your friend Diego

4. On the spaghetti sauce and cheese were heaped.

5. Betty Hoskins Ph.D. conducts nutrition research for Snacks Unlimited Inc.

6. Before we lived at 12436 South Princeton Street.

7. One famous address is 1600 Pennsylvania Avenue Washington D.C.

8. On July 20 1969 Neil Armstrong became the first human to set foot on the moon.

9. The information operator for ZIP code 02114 received 5200 calls last month.

10. Donald Burke M.D. of Superalloy Inc. is an industrial medicine specialist.

11. The house at 35 Beale Street Brookline Massachusetts is John F. Kennedy's birthplace.

12. The interior temperature of a star can be as high as 1100000°C.

13. Katerina won a gold metal; Debi a bronze.

14. Maria asked for she was the only one who spoke Greek.

15. Was Martin Luther King Jr. assassinated in July 1968?

Commas: Other Uses

A. Using Commas

The following passage tests many of the comma rules you have learned. Add commas where they are needed.

On February 14 1988 I bought my first antique marble. Now I'm an avid collector. Anyone who likes collecting marbles should consider joining the Marble Collectors Society of America. There are about 3000 members. With your membership you receive a set of pictures illustrating 380 different marbles a newsletter that tells of auctions and marble fairs and a pricing guide. The Marble Collectors Society has set up good exhibits of marbles at the Smithsonian in Washington D.C.; the Corning Glass Museum in Corning New York; and the Museum of Glass in Milleville New Jersey.

The prices of marbles have gone up dramatically in the last several years. In 1978 sulphides those with figures or portraits inside sold for $50 to $110. Now they go for $300 to $2000. Lutz marbles those with gold stone flecks sell for $30 to $100. Peppermint swirls can sell for up to $100. To buyers high prices bring frowns; low prices smiles. There are still many common marbles to buy for ten cents apiece.

B. Using Commas

Insert commas where they are needed. Cross out any comma that is not necessary.

The Pony Express was a mail delivery service, that operated between St. Joseph Missouri and Sacramento California. It began its first run on April 3 1860. Its relays of men riding ponies carried letters, across a trail 1966 miles (3164 kilometers) long.

It usually took the Pony Express about ten days to make the run between St. Joseph Missouri and Sacramento California. The fastest run happened in March, 1861. A copy of an address to Congress by Abraham Lincoln President of the United States was delivered in seven and one-half days.

The transcontinental telegraph, opened on October 24 1861. In short delivery by the Pony Express was no longer the fastest means of communicating with the West. The Pony Express closed two days later. Its investors lost over $100000.

These days there are many successors to the Pony Express and the telegraph. The U.S. Postal Service and several private companies offer "fast-mail" deliveries. For example, a letter or package sent late in the afternoon of one day from Atlanta Georgia will be delivered to an address in Seattle Washington the next morning; to an address overseas the morning after that. Radio TV the telephone and the computer of course are even more impressive. From one place to another anywhere on earth they can communicate information instantaneously.

Semicolons separate different elements in a sentence. When there are several commas within parts of a compound sentence, use a semicolon to separate the parts.

> Kim writes, paints, and acts; and she is a talented musician.

When there are commas within parts of a series, use a semicolon to separate the parts.

> We visited Oslo, Norway; Rome, Italy; and Paris, France.

Use a semicolon to join the parts of a compound sentence that are not joined by a coordinating conjunction such as *and* or *but*.

> The silkworm is not a worm; it is a caterpillar.

Use a semicolon before a conjunctive adverb or a parenthetical expression that joins the clauses of a compound sentence.

> Braque was an innovative artist; in fact, he helped to develop cubism.

Using the Semicolon

Insert semicolons where necessary in these sentences.

1. The map included Washington, Oregon, and Idaho but Alaska was not shown.

2. Sri Lanka is noted for tea, rubies, and rubber it was formerly Ceylon.

3. In the Northern Hemisphere, winter lasts from December to March in the Southern Hemisphere, it lasts from June to December.

4. Huang Ho, China's Yellow River, floods often in fact, one million people were killed when it flooded in 1887.

5. Boise, Idaho Juneau, Alaska and Des Moines, Iowa, are state capitals.

6. Andrew Young was once our ambassador to the United Nations and he then became Mayor of Atlanta, Georgia.

7. Martha loves music however, she never learned to play an instrument.

8. The choir toured London, England Hamburg, Germany and Milan, Italy.

9. Li was in charge of the rally Bo, the parade and Ana, the dance.

10. The banker opened the old, rusted, and abandoned safe but he found it empty.

11. My sisters were born on June 4, 1979 August 2, 1981 and April 3, 1986.

12. Tweed is a woolen fabric it was originally made by weavers in Tweed, Scotland.

13. Integrated circuits have made the miniaturization of many electronic devices possible in short, they have revolutionized the electronics industry.

14. Today Venezuela is one of the world's leading exporters of petroleum before the 1920's Venezuela exported only cacao and coffee.

15. Bruges, Belgium, has long been famous for its lace in fact, it is one of the few places in Belgium where lace is still made by hand.

The Semicolon

A. Using the Semicolon
Insert semicolons where necessary in these sentences.

1. On February 25, 1986, Corazon Aquino became the president of the Philippines Ferdinand Marcos had resigned the presidency and fled the country.

2. The population of Massachusetts is approximately 6,823,000 of California, 26,366,000 and of New York, 17,785,000.

3. Ronald Reagan was born in 1911 he became our fortieth President.

4. China has the world's largest population however, the government strongly promotes a policy of one child per family.

5. The capital of California, the most highly populated state, is Sacramento and San Francisco and Los Angeles are California's most famous cities.

6. Richard Nixon was elected to two terms as President of the United States he did not complete the second term.

7. Vulcanization was invented by Charles Goodyear it is a process of treating crude rubber by subjecting it to intense heat in order to make it strong.

8. Woody Guthrie was a folk singer his best-known song is "This Land Is Your Land."

9. W. C. Handy was an American composer he wrote some of the earliest blues songs.

B. Using the Semicolon in Writing
Insert semicolons where they are needed in the following paragraphs.

(1) Frostbite is dangerous, the skin and tissue can actually freeze as a result of exposure to intense cold. (2) Frostbite can occur in many parts of the body, but it most often affects the ears, nose, fingers, and toes.

(3) In the early stages of frostbite, the skin appears red, pain is often present. (4) As the condition develops, the skin turns gray-white, and the pain disappears, at this stage it is easy to treat. (5) A person who has frostbite should cover the exposed area with warm gloves then they should get out of the cold. (6) When the person is indoors, he or she should remove all tight, wet clothing, immerse the area in warm, not hot, water, and cover the affected area loosely with warm, dry clothes. (7) The person should not warm the frostbitten area by sitting near a flame or radiator, this heat might burn the skin. (8) He or she should not massage the area, massage might damage frozen tissues. (9) The victim should not break any blisters, doing so could increase the chance of infection.

(10) People who go out in the cold can prevent frostbite precautions are simple. (11) If they expect to be out a long time, they should wear warm, nonconstricting clothing, hikers should take along extra clothing.

The Colon

The **colon** is used to direct the reader's attention forward to what follows. Use a colon to introduce a list of items, a quotation that lacks explanatory words such as *he said* or *she asked*, or a very long or very formal quotation.

> The following countries are in the Balkans: Greece, Albania, and Bulgaria. Antony began his speech by saying: "Friends, Romans, countrymen, lend me your ears; I come to bury Caesar, not to praise him."

Use a colon between two independent clauses when the second explains the first.

> The skiers cheered for joy: three feet of new snow had fallen overnight.

Also use a colon (1) after the formal salutation of a business letter, (2) between the hour and minute figures of clock time, (3) in Biblical references to indicate the chapter and verse, (4) between the title and subtitle of a book, (5) between the numbers referring to the volume and pages of books and magazines, and (6) after labels that signal important ideas.

> Dear Ms. Jones:
> Please meet me in my office at 7:30 A.M. next Monday. We will review *The Shopping Mall High School: Winners and Losers in the Educational Marketplace* and Leon Edel's *Henry James,* Volume I: 126-132.
> Note: This is a very important meeting.

Using the Colon

Insert colons where needed in the following sentences.

1. Does the train leave at 715 A.M. or 815 A.M.?

2. *A Tale of Two Cities* begins with this famous sentence "It was the best of times, it was the worst of times."

3. We knew that Sybil Wright would win the contest she sang beautifully.

4. Take all the rain gear we expect bad weather.

5. This month's movies include the following *Shane, Casablanca, Raiders of the Lost Ark,* and *Alien.*

6. Warning May cause drowsiness.

7. Julius Caesar is famous for his concise statement "I came, I saw, I conquered."

8. I must get up at 700 A.M. to catch the bus.

9. Our map was inadequate it did not indicate the steep slopes and sharp curves that we would meet.

10. To Whom It May Concern
    I am writing to request a refund.

11. Postal workers deliver mail in all types of weather rain, sleet, snow, and hail.

12. The class reading assignment is Volume 1 13-21 and volume 2 71-73.

13. The tallest of animals is the giraffe its legs alone measure six feet.

14. I enjoyed the book *Belle Boyd The Life of a Confederate Spy.*

15. Attention This beach closes at dusk.

A. Using the Colon
Insert colons as needed in the following sentences.

1. It was Virginia Woolf who wrote these words "Anonymous was a woman."
2. The following plays are classified as tragedies *Macbeth, Othello,* and *King Lear.*
3. These animals are mollusks, squid, snails, and limpets.
4. Our neighbors posted a sign Beware of the Dog.
5. My train for school leaves at 655 A.M. and arrives at 750 A.M.
6. Jim's essay referred to *National Geographic,* Vol. 143 318-319.
7. During World War II, to express his nation's gratitude to its brave Royal Air Force pilots, British Prime Minister Winston Churchill said "Never in the field of human conflict was so much owed by so many to so few."
8. Winter is not the season for planting spring is a better time.
9. Susan wrote a short story entitled "The Maypole A Story of Folk Dancing."
10. Theo came to a decision he would apply for that job after all.
11. Did you read the article in *Smithsonian,* Vol. 18 88-99?
12. Beware Guard dogs are on duty.

B. Using the Colon in Writing
Insert colons where they are needed in the following paragraphs.

(1) Fire experts say you have one minute to get out of a house after the smoke detector goes off. (2) In five minutes a two-story house is fully ablaze fire breaks through the roof, and flames curl from every window. (3) There's no time to do the things that most people think they would do, which include the following collect valuables, get dressed, and call the fire department. (4) That's because fire is explosive as temperatures build and gases accumulate, things don't burn; they blow up.

(5) Tyrone Judkins knows how fast fire spreads. (6) On May 23, at 400 A.M., his smoke detector blared. (7) Judkins recalls "Flames shot up the wall like a bonfire." (8) He tried an old fire extinguisher, but the gauge read "Warning Low Pressure." (9) It was useless. (10) A fireball raced down the hall to the bedrooms. (11) Fortunately, his family was safe they had escaped through the bedroom windows. (12) Just before he jumped out of the window, he glanced at the clock; 403 was the time. (13) In three minutes the whole house was afire. (14) Luckily, Tyrone and his family had read the book *Fire How to Survive One.* (15) It may have saved all of their lives.

The Dash

Dashes are used to indicate an abrupt change of thought or a pause in a sentence. Use a dash to set off a long explanatory statement that interrupts the main thought, to set off parenthetical expressions that show an abrupt break in thought, or to set off a summarizing statement from the rest of the sentence.

> Norden—not Scandinavia alone but also Finland and Iceland—has a rich literature of myth and folklore.
> In the 1920's the Algonquin Hotel—the building is still standing today—was the meeting place of a group of famous writers.
> Anemones, jonquils, freesias, lilies—these were in the bride's bouquet.

When writing dialogue, use a dash to show an abrupt break in thought.

> "Domesday Book—do you know about that?—was an early census."

A. Using the Dash
Underline the words that should be set off with a dash or dashes.

1. That vacation I'll give you details later was unbelievable!

2. Ann can't practice her favorite sports skiing, volley ball, and golf because of an injury.

3. Giant pandas, peregrine falcons, and Bali leopards these are endangered species.

4. "First, let me show you oh, you already know how!"

5. Measles, mumps, and whooping cough common childhood illnesses fifty years ago are now controlled by immunization.

B. Using the Dash
Rewrite each sentence inserting dashes where they belong. Note that a dash (—) is longer than a hyphen (-).

1. Solids, liquids, and gases we worked with all three in chemistry class. _____

_____

2. "The book ends with no, you should read the ending yourself." _____

_____

3. This gem perhaps the most extraordinary in the world contains no flaw. _____

_____

4. The Eskimos they call themselves *Inuit* or *Yuit* live in the Arctic. _____

_____

5. Buteos, kites, falcons all more commonly called hawks frequent our region. _____

_____

The Dash

A. Using the Dash

Rewrite each sentence, inserting the words in parentheses in an appropriate place and setting them off with a dash or dashes.

1. They're going to give him first prize. (this is in strict confidence)

   _____

2. Pumpkin and sunflower seeds are really delicious. (you can roast them yourself)

   _____

3. Amber was once thought to have healing properties. (few know that it is the fossilized resin of certain evergreens)

   _____

4. The cashier said, "That will be seven dollars." (no, I have to add extra for tax)

   _____

5. The platypus is indigenous to Australia. (a very strange-looking animal and a mysterious presence in the landscape)

   _____

B. Using the Dash in Writing

Indicate where dashes are needed in the following paragraphs by writing them in the space above the words to be separated.

Porcupines are interesting animals. They can be divided into two groups, Old World porcupines and New World porcupines. Most Old World porcupines they live in Africa, parts of Asia, Indian, and southern Europe are about three feet long.

One Old World species of porcupine it is a large animal up to sixty pounds with an array of sharp quills on its back and tail has been found in northern Africa and southern Europe. These quills effective defensive and offensive weapons have backward-pointing barbs. When an enemy approaches, the porcupine stamps its feet and rattles its quills. If this warning is disregarded a dangerous mistake for the enemy the porcupine attacks, running backward at high speed. It stabs its enemy with the quills of its rump, and this action is like the sting of a bee the barbs become embedded in the enemy's skin. This method of attack helps to explain the legend it's still believed by some that the porcupine can shoot its quills at an enemy.

The Hyphen

Use a hyphen in compound numbers from twenty-one to ninety-nine, in fractions that are spelled out and used as adjectives, and in certain compound words.

    fifty-three   one-eighth part   jack-in-the-box   by-product

Use a hyphen between words that make up a compound adjective used before a noun and with some proper nouns and proper adjectives with suffixes and prefixes.

    up-tight person   pre-Raphaelite   well-known author   Pan-Americanism

Use a hyphen if part of a word must be carried over from one line to the next.

    In medieval castles in Europe the keep is the strongest, inner-
        most part of the central tower.

Using the Hyphen
Insert the hyphens where they belong in the following sentences.

1. Despite a crippled leg in her childhood, Wilma Rudolph became a world class runner.

2. Rocky Bleier, with only two thirds use of his disabled right foot and leg, helped carry the Pittsburgh Steelers to four Super Bowls.

3. Louisa May Alcott wrote the best selling novel *Little Women*.

4. Fifteen year old Upton Sinclair supported his family by selling stories to maga zines.

5. Darla Hood, an American movie actress, made forty eight *Our Gang* comedies.

6. Well known writer Barbara Cartland writes about twenty books a year.

7. Italian dictator Benito Mussolini was pro German during World War II.

8. The Russian born painter Wassily Kandinsky belonged to the expressionist school of painting.

9. The award winning novel *The Bone People*, which is set in New Zealand, was written by Keri Hume.

10. The world renowned Mexican author Carlos Fuentes published his first book, *Where the Air Is Clear*, in 1958.

11. Playwright Athol Fugard, who is South African, is known for the anti apartheid themes of his plays.

12. Post impressionist painters like Cézanne and Seurat were convinced that im pressionism would not have lasting value as an art form.

13. During the 1970's the Montreal Canadiens of the National Hockey League were six time winners of the Stanley Cup.

14. Did you know Mikhail Baryshnikov was a soloist with the Kirov Ballet in Russia be fore he defected to the West in 1974?

15. The Congo River, the fifth longest river in the world, has no delta.

The Hyphen

A. Using the Hyphen
Add hyphens where necessary in the following sentences.

1. Daylight saving time, which the British adopted in World War I, provides additional evening light for summer activities.
2. Frances Parkinson Keyes's best known work, *Dinner at Antoine's,* is a murder mystery set in New Orleans.
3. Ex Governor General Warren Hastings, who was once a clerk with the East India Company, was impeached for corruption.
4. During the spring and summer of 1987, many people in the United States viewed the Iran Contra hearings on television.
5. Court ordered school desegregation in certain cities in the northern states of the United States began in 1973.
6. The Heye Foundation in New York City displays a collection of pre Columbian art.

B. Using the Hyphen in Writing
Insert hyphens where they are needed in the following paragraphs.

Montana's nicknames—the Treasure State and Big Sky Country—truly de scribes its character. Its main treasure is gold and silver. In 1889, rich strikes of these ores led to an expansion in population. Later, other sought after minerals were added to the treasure—copper, oil, zinc, and even gem sapphires. Montana's treasure is also found in its ever present herds of cattle and sheep, in its yellow gold fields of grain, and in the high energy flow of its rivers.

The Big Sky Country is well named because Montana is immense. Only Alaska, Texas, and California have larger areas. Montana, despite its size, is forty fourth in population. There is a lot of "living" room under the Big Sky.

The state takes its name from the Spanish word meaning "mountain." Actually, only the western third of Montana is mountainous; the remaining two thirds consists of gently rolling terrain with wide horizons.

The inhabitants of Montana are well known for their fierce love of the state's sprawling and beautiful land with its vast, open out of doors. Visitors to the state, observing the snow capped mountain peaks, swift flowing streams, and abundant forests, find the natives' sentiments fully justified.

158 *Handbook 40 Semicolons, Colons, and Other Punctuation*

Parentheses

Use parentheses to set off supplementary or explanatory material that is loosely joined to the sentence.

> Robin Hood, a legendary English outlaw (many scholars believe he is a fictitious character), stood as a symbol of "right against might."

Use parentheses to enclose figures or letters in a list that is part of a sentence.

> We were told to (1) run a mile, (2) jump a stile, and (3) climb a tree.

Use parentheses to informally identify a source of information you use in your writing or to give credit to an author whose ideas or words you are using.

> "The English Language surrounds us like a sea, and like the waters of the deep, it is full of mysteries" (McCrum, Cran, and MacNeil, *The Story of English*).

Use punctuation marks inside the parentheses when they belong to the parenthetical material. When punctuation marks belong to the main part of the sentence, place them outside of the parentheses.

> I didn't know (did you?) that paper was invented in China.
> Ana barbecued the chicken (her favorite meal); Eric made the salads.

Using Parentheses

Insert parentheses where they belong in the following sentences.

1. Underline and identify a the subject, b the verb, and c the complement.

2. I'm sure aren't you? that Marcia will get the job.

3. "There is a new spirit abroad among women today" Miller, p. ix.

4. The election campaign more detail later took all our energy.

5. Lou Gehrig 1903-1941 was known as the Pride of the Yankees.

6. The word *funambulist* tightrope walker has a Latin derivation.

7. Kahlil Gibran's *The Prophet* it's still popular was written in 1923.

8. I saw Mr. Perry remember him? at the sporting goods shop yesterday.

9. The committee includes Senator Bar Democrat and Senator Holt Republican.

10. England, Scotland, and Wales I was in Wales last August are known collectively as Great Britain.

11. Cary Grant he was great in *To Catch A Thief* was born in England.

12. *A Summons to Memphis* did you ever get around to reading it? is the book for which Peter Taylor won the Pulitzer Prize in 1987.

13. I received the check you were right! in the mail yesterday.

14. Before the truck will run, you will need to a rebuild the carburetor, b replace the alternator, and c install a battery.

15. "The past is a foreign country; they do things differently there" L. P. Hartley, *The Go-Between*.

Parentheses

A. Using Parentheses
Rewrite each sentence, inserting parentheses where appropriate.

1. Massachusetts its nickname is the Bay State became the sixth state in the Union in 1788.

   _____

2. The ship *Queen Elizabeth 2* is 963 feet 294 meters long.

   _____

3. Founded in 1648, the French Academy attempts to keep the French language free of too much foreign influence see related article on page 589.

   _____

4. The Republican Party GOP has a smaller membership than does the Democratic Party, the other major political party in the United States.

   _____

   _____

B. Using Parentheses in Writing
Add parentheses where they are needed in the following paragraphs.

Bessie Smith 1894-1937 was the Empress of the Blues. She was born in Chattanooga, Tennessee, one of seven children. She never knew her Baptist-minister father he died shortly after her birth, and barely knew her mother she died when Bessie was eight. At age nine Bessie made her debut on the streets of Chattanooga, singing for nickels and dimes.

Bessie's first recording 1923 was "Down Hearted Blues," a great success. The song still alive and well sparked near-riots at her performances and established her with an almost legendary reputation.

Then Bessie recorded "St. Louis Blues" 1929 about a woman who is two-timed by her handsome "gamblin' man." It was a restrained yet powerful collaboration of three major talents: W. C. Handy composer, Bessie Smith vocalist, and Louis Armstrong cornet. The song had a structure of three themes: a a twelve-measure blues section; b a sixteen-measure section, usually done as a tango; and c the main twelve-measure blues section. It is this song ask any blues lover for which Bessie Smith is most remembered.

Apostrophes (I)

Use apostrophes to form the **possessive** of singular and plural nouns. To form the possessive of a singular noun, add an apostrophe and an *s* even if the noun ends in *s*.

> aunt's   man's   Bess's

To form the possessive of a plural noun that ends in *s* or *es,* add an apostrophe. Form the possessive of a plural noun that does not end in *s* by adding an apostrophe and an *s.*

> aunts'   men's   the Rodgers'

To form the possessive of a compound noun, add an apostrophe and an *s* only to the last part of the noun.

> brother-in-law's hat   town clerk's job

In the case of joint ownership, only the name of the last person mentioned is given the possessive form. Add an apostrophe or an apostrophe and *s,* depending on the spelling of the name. This rule also applies to the possessives of the names of organizations.

> Sandra and Linda's house   National Food Store's policy

If the names of two or more persons are used to show separate ownership, each name is given the possessive form.

> Jack's and Kent's jackets   Revere's and Lynn's locations

Using Apostrophes

In the blanks, write the correct possessive form of the boldfaced words.

1. **Anthony** and **Jeremy** responsibility was cleaning the fish tank. _____

2. What are the **National Music Camp** requirements for admission? _____

3. The **Morgans** and **Swansons** cars were damaged in the collision. _____

4. **Passengers** complaints about the two-hour delay did no good. _____

5. The **gallery** collection of Eskimo art is marvelous. _____

6. Local journalists are attending an **editors** conference. _____

7. My **brother-in-law** attention was distracted by the singing. _____

8. The **sopranos** duet was fine, but the **tenor** solo was weak. _____

9. The **men** shoes in that store are all imported from Italy. _____

10. The Pyrenees form **Spain** northern border. _____

11. Jane is knitting sweaters from wool she bought at **Jordan** and **Jackson** sale. _____

12. The **children** instructors had recommended them for advanced classes. _____

Apostrophes (I)

A. Using Apostrophes

Underline the words that should be possessives in the following sentences. Write the correct forms in the space above them.

1. Rodgers and Hart collaboration produced many wonderful show tunes.

2. Philip Glass music has been used in many theatrical productions.

3. Albert Einstein theory of relativity revolutionized scientific conceptions of time, space, mass, and motion.

4. The debaters meeting will be held at four o'clock.

5. Chicago and St. Louis bids for the Worlds Fair were considered.

6. The cities advantages include excellent public transportation systems.

7. The waiter tips for the day were large, and his boss face broke into a smile.

8. Miranda, Ariel, and Oberon are the names of three of Uranus fifteen moons.

B. Using Apostrophes in Paragraphs

Write the correct forms of the possessives in the space above them in the following paragraphs.

(1) Famed artist Marc Chagalls paintings are fantasies. (2) His paintings images include walking fish and violin-playing cows, among others. (3) A hard worker, Chagall turned out more than three thousand paintings, as well as stage sets and costumes, sculptures, and stained-glass windows.

(4) Chagalls roots were in Russia, where he was born in 1887. (5) In 1910, as a young man in Paris, he painted to his hearts content, using bed sheets as canvases. (6) His paintings style made him famous. (7) In 1950, he moved to the south of France, where he lived until his death in 1985 at the age of 97.

(8) No one has a style quite like Chagalls. (9) His paintings bold, solid shapes and colors—burning reds, juicy greens, and magic blues—jump off the canvases. (10) When Chagalls ideas for paintings began to diminish, he turned to stained glass; in a few years he made hundreds of stained-glass windows. (11) One of his windows is in the General Assembly Building of the United Nations in New York City.

Apostrophes (II)

To form the possessive of an indefinite pronoun, add an apostrophe and *s*.

> everybody's   no one's

Add an apostrophe and *s* to the last word to form the possessives of compound pronouns.

> everybody else's term paper   no one else's reason

Do not use an apostrophe with a personal pronoun to show possession.

> Is this letter yours?   Its envelope is missing.

When nouns expressing time and amount are used as adjectives, they are given the possessive form.

> a year's wait   three hours' pay

Use an apostrophe in a contraction.

> she's   you'll   couldn't

Use an apostrophe to show the omission of figures.

> class of '81   the crash of '87

Use apostrophes to form the plurals of letters, numbers, signs, and words referred to as words.

> How many *s*'s are in your name?
> He used too many *if*'s in his talk.
> Saddle shoes were popular in the *1940*'s.

Using Apostrophes

In the blanks, write the correct forms of the boldfaced words including apostrophes. If no apostrophe is needed, write **Correct**.

1. *Wasnt* basketball originally played with a peach basket instead of a net? _____

2. The car Jim bought is a *67* Mustang. _____

3. Rachel's house is just ten *minutes* walk from mine. _____

4. The use of videos and computers skyrocketed in the *1980's.* _____

5. *Shell* be in the city in one hour. _____

6. Be sure you dot your *is* in your papers. _____

7. The Wilson family had gone to the World's Fair of *84.* _____

8. Last *years* historical events were full of political surprises. _____

9. Our poor harvest from the vegetable garden is *nobodys* fault. _____

10. The door squeaked; *its* hinges were rusty. _____

Apostrophes (II)

A. Using Apostrophes

Underline the words and other items that should contain apostrophes. Write the correct forms in the space above them.

1. Manny lost points on the math test; all his 2s looked like 3s.

2. Nellie Bly was twenty-two when she made her seventy-two days journey around the world in 1889.

3. Kristin Azzarello has two *is*, two *as*, two *ls*, and two *zs* in her name.

4. You mustnt worry about things beyond your control.

5. Eleven oclock in England is known as elevenses, time for a tea break.

6. Ms. Woods graduated from college with the class of 81.

7. Dont you know that February 12 is Abraham Lincolns birthday?

8. Walker Percy is a wonderful writer; no one elses books affect me the way his do.

9. Luis returned Anas book but kept yours.

10. Shes such a good photographer that she might win a Pulitzer Prize.

B. Using Apostrophes in Paragraphs

Underline the words and other items that should contain apostrophes in the following paragraphs. Write the correct forms in the space above them.

(1) No ones summer vacation would be better than mine. (2) Within a months time Id be on my way to Coastline Photography Institute to take a photography course. (3) Whats so great, some might ask, about such an institute? (4) Its a special place, I say.

(5) This summer the class of 91 will be studying the following topics: The Three *P*s of Photography; The Camera—Making It Everyones Best Friend; Pictures Youll Be Proud to Display; and The Camera—Changes Since the 1950s. (6) Our grades will depend on the quality of our photographs.

(7) The coursework isnt the only interesting part of the institute. (8) Last year everyones work was displayed. (9) Its worth a years wait to see the work of classmates. (10) Some people sell their work; everybody elses is returned after the photography showing.

Quotation Marks (I)

Use quotation marks to begin and end a direct quotation. In a **direct quotation,** the words of the speaker are quoted exactly, and the first word of the quotation is capitalized.

> **Direct Quotation**   Lionel said, "I would like to play tennis."

Both parts of a **divided quotation** are enclosed in quotation marks. The first word of the second part of the quotation is not capitalized unless it begins a new sentence.

> **Divided Quotations** "I would like to play tennis," said Lionel, "but I can't."
> "I would like to play tennis," said Lionel. "Do you?"

Quotation marks are never used with an **indirect quotation,** which reports the meaning of the speaker but not the exact words.

> **Indirect Quotation**   Lionel said that he would like to play tennis.

When the end of the quotation is also the end of the sentence, the period falls inside the quotation marks. If the quotation is a question or an exclamation, the question mark or exclamation point falls inside the quotation marks. If the entire sentence that contains the quotation is a question or an exclamation, the question mark or exclamation point falls outside the quotation marks. Also note the placement of commas to set the quotation apart from the rest of the sentence.

> The crowd yelled, "Hurray!"   Did you say, "Come in"?

Single quotation marks are used to enclose a quotation within a quotation.

> He asked, "Who said the words, 'Give me liberty or give me death'?"

A new paragraph and a new set of quotation marks show a change in speaker.

Using Quotation Marks

Insert the necessary punctuation and underline any words that should be capitalized. If the sentence is punctuated correctly, write **Correct** in the blank.

1. The whole secret of the study of nature wrote George Sand lies in learning how

   to use one's eyes. _____

2. When Archimedes discovered the natural law of buoyancy, he exclaimed eureka! _____

3. Muhammad Ali said my famous saying is float like a butterfly, sting like a bee. _____

4. Edna St. Vincent Millay wrote time can make soft that iron wood. _____

5. Zachary asked why no one had given him a surprise party. _____

6. Five weeks is too long to live out of a suitcase the girl replied. _____

7. Do not count your chickens before they are hatched warned Aesop. _____

8. Mr. Osada said to read Chapter 10 for tomorrow. _____

9. This dress is incredible exclaimed Rosa. You've never seen one like it! _____

10. Did the policewoman say that a child in a red sweatshirt is lost? _____

Quotation Marks (I)

A. Using Quotation Marks
Insert the necessary punctuation and underline any words that should be capitalized in the following paragraphs.

The National Severe Storms Forecast Center in Kansas City, Missouri, accurately predicted yesterday's thunderstorms. Gus Pappas, director of the center said the thunder seemed loud enough to split my house apart. The lightning bolts that lit up the sky were the largest I've ever seen. Asked if he was a little scared during the storm, he replied weren't you?

Pappas gave several precautions you can use to protect yourself from lightning. If possible he said get indoors and stay there. Avoid open doors and windows, fireplaces, and metal items. Do not touch plugged-in appliances, including the telephone he continued. If you are outside, avoid the highest object in the area. The Water Safety manual states stay off small boats and out of the water. My advice is to get on the ground fast if you feel your hair standing up! Lightning may be about to strike you.

Pappas had many excellent tips to give the audience regarding the precautions one should take during lightning storms. He said that it was best to be informed. Only then he added can you take the precautions that might save your life.

B. Using Quotation Marks in Writing
Insert the necessary punctuation and underline any words that should be capitalized in the following dialogue.

Listen, do you hear that thunder asked Emilio. I'd better go before the lightning starts.

Didn't you know that if we can hear thunder, lightning has already struck asked Tim.

Emilio thought about what Tim had said. Then he asked Tim where he had gotten his information.

Tim answered I clearly remember that this is what the *World Book Encyclopedia* says: scientists know that the sound of thunder is caused by the violent expansion of air that has been heated by lightning. He added that means that the lightning has to come first; don't you agree?

In that case said Emilio I'll just stay here until the storm is over.

Use quotation marks to enclose the titles of chapters, stories, short poems, essays, articles, television episodes, and short musical compositions.

> You'd like James Plunkett's short story "The Half-Crown."
> "Youth and Age" is a poem by the Irish writer Eleanor Hull.

Use quotation marks to set off words used in special ways and to set off slang.

> Ben calls the people of our town the "locals."

When a word and its definition appear in a sentence, the word is italicized (or underlined) and the definition is in quotation marks.

> The word *ingress* means "entrance."

Using Quotation Marks

Insert the necessary punctuation in each of the following sentences. Underline any words that would be italicized in type.

1. The world enthrall means to enslave.

2. Have you ever read Dorothy Parker's poem Surprise?

3. To Build a Fire is the name of a short story by Jack London.

4. There are several short stories I would recommend, such as Lilacs.

5. In the book *The Asians* I was especially interested in the chapter The Japanese Woman and the chapter Politics in Japan.

6. The word chortle, meaning to utter with a snorting sound, was coined by Lewis Carroll.

7. My mother calls the water fountain the bubbler.

8. The word dollop means a lump or a large portion.

9. I know you'd like Robert Frost's poem Birches.

10. Have you read Shirley Jackson's short story The Lottery?

11. What does the word ambivalent mean?

12. In British English a truck is called a lorry.

13. The poem Lucinda Matlock, from Edgar Lee Master's book *Spoon River Anthology*, ends with the line, "It takes life to love Life."

14. Do you know what poet wrote the poem The Hollow Men?

15. I made up humorous new words for the song I've Been Workin' on the Railroad.

16. Charles Lamb's essay, A Dissertation Upon Roast Pig, humorously explains why pork is cooked.

17. One meaning of the word lark is harmless fun.

18. Artistic use of lasers is described in the article Painting with Light.

19. Our cousins in the country call a small stream a crick.

20. He used the word railed to mean complained bitterly.

Quotation Marks (II)

Using Quotation Marks

Rewrite the following sentences, using correct punctuation. When a word and its definition appear, be sure to underline the word.

1. The Latin phrase quo vadis means Where are you going?

   _____

2. This paragraph is from the chapter called Flood in Annie Dillard's book *Pilgrim at Tinker Creek*.

   _____

   _____

3. Edgar Allan Poe wrote beautiful, haunting poems; among them are The Raven and

   Annabel Lee. _____

   _____

4. Rachel Carson wrote the essay Wind and Water.

   _____

5. Have you ever heard the Irish folk song The Wind That Shakes the Barley?

   _____

6. Exempli gratia is a Latin phrase meaning for example.

   _____

7. Earvin Johnson is called Magic because of the amazing moves he makes on the basketball court.

   _____

   _____

8. I didn't know that the word egregious meant flagrant.

   _____

9. The twins call their dog the garbage can because he will eat anything.

   _____

10. Bob Dylan wrote the 1960's protest song Blowin' in the Wind.

    _____

Directions One or more of the underlined sections in the following sentences may contain errors of grammar, usage, punctuation, spelling, or capitalization. Write the letter of each incorrect section; then rewrite the item correctly. If there is no error in an item, write *E.* Write your answers on your own paper or on an answer sheet, as your teacher directs.

Example   The <u>milky way, which is</u> made up of billions of <u>stars can</u> be
                A   **B**   **C**
easily seen as bright haze on a clear <u>summer</u> night. <u>No error</u>
                                       D   **E**

Answer   A—Milky Way   C—stars, can

1. In a ship named *Half Moon*, Henry Hudson explored Chesapeake Bay,
                  A
<u>Delaware Bay,</u> and the <u>Hudson river</u> <u>in 1609.</u> <u>No error</u>
  B   **C**   **D**   **E**

2. Horace Greeley was a <u>nineteenth century</u> newspaper publisher, <u>abolitionist,</u> and
                          A   **B**
<u>politician:</u> he popularized the phrase "Go west, young <u>man."</u> <u>No error</u>
  C   **D**   **E**

3. The word *savvy* means <u>"knowledgeable:"</u> it comes from the <u>Spanish</u> verb *saber,*
          A   **B**   **C**
meaning <u>"to know."</u> <u>No error</u>
        D   **E**

4. After observing a <u>persons</u> attempt to imitate <u>her,</u> <u>Queen Victoria</u> of England
                    A   **B**   **C**
declared, "We are not <u>amused".</u> <u>No error</u>
                  D   **E**

5. A sloth—<u>among humans the name describes a very lazy person</u>—is a slow-
                              A
moving <u>South American</u> animal that <u>hardly ever</u> leaves <u>its</u> treetop home. <u>No error</u>
        B   **C**   **D**   **E**

6. In his poem <u>"Mending Wall,"</u> Robert Frost <u>writes:</u> "Something there is that doesn't
                    A   **B**
love a <u>wall"; however,</u> the same poem <u>states: "Good</u> fences make good
         C   **D**
neighbors." <u>No error</u>
           E

7. The <u>vedas</u> are the most ancient texts of the <u>Hindu religion;</u> composed

      A   **B**

   about <u>1000 B.C.,</u> these teachings had great influence on <u>Indian culture.</u> <u>No error</u>

          C   **D**   **E**

8. <u>Mrs. Vallejo, I</u> can assure you that the <u>editor-in-chiefs</u> face was not <u>smiling</u>

    A   **B**   **C**

   when he saw the date <u>July 27, 1771</u> on the front page of today's newspaper.

                      D

   <u>No error</u>

     E

9. The <u>*viking II* space craft</u> landed on <u>Mars</u> on <u>September 3, 1976;</u> it analyzed the

           A   **B**   **C**

   soil and <u>atmosphere,</u> and sent back photographs. <u>No error</u>

             D   **E**

10. Should I write to the <u>Director of Admissions and Registrar,</u> United States Military

                                       A

   Academy, <u>West Point,</u> <u>NY 10996,</u> for information about admission <u>policys?</u>

                B   **C**   **D**

   <u>No error</u>

     E

11. Do you remember <u>which American</u> leader <u>said,</u> <u>"The only</u> thing we have to fear is

                   A   **B**   **C**

   fear <u>itself?"</u> <u>No error</u>

       D   **E**

12. <u>Henry James,</u> the author of <u>*Portrait of a Lady,*</u> was the brother of the

      A   **B**

   philosopher <u>William James,</u> author of <u>*The Varieties of Religious Experience.*</u>

               C   **D**

   <u>No error</u>

     E

13. <u>Willem Kolff M.D.</u> of the <u>University of Utah was</u> the first <u>doctor</u> to implant an

      A   **B**   **C**

   artificial <u>human heart; the</u> recipient of the heart was Barney Clark. <u>No error</u>

            D   **E**

14. Did you know that <u>senator Robert J. Dole</u> of <u>Kansas</u> once tried to win

                    A   **B**

   the <u>Republican party's</u> nomination for <u>President?</u> <u>No error</u>

        C   **D**   **E**

15. <u>The Declaration of Independence,</u> <u>the Constitution,</u> and <u>the Bill of Rights</u> are the

            A   **B**   **C**

   three most important documents in <u>American history.</u> <u>No error</u>

                                  D   **E**

Directions Read the passage and choose the word or group of words that belongs in each numbered space. Write the letter of the correct answer on your own paper or on an answer sheet, as your teacher directs.

Example   At the height of the ___(1)___, 13 million Americans were out of work. To provide jobs, President Roosevelt proposed these agencies ___(2)___ the Civilian Conservation Corps, the Works Progress Administration, and the Farm Credit Administration.

1. A. great depression
    B. Great Depression
    C. Great depression
    D. great Depression

2. A. agencies,
    B. agencies;
    C. agencies:
    D. agencies.

Answer   1—B   2—C

Long before the beginning of the ___(16)___ many citizens felt that the new nation should be named Columbia, after the ___(17)___ Christopher Columbus. The word *Columbia* ___(18)___ was used by the African-American poet Phyllis Wheatley to refer to America. Another poet of the time, Philip Freneau, popularized the word in his poem ___(19)___ Throughout the war, the name *Columbia* was used to express ___(20)___ desire for an independent homeland. Later, many towns in the young nation adopted the name, including Columbia, ___(21)___.

16. A. revolutionary War,
    B. Revolutionary war
    C. Revolutionary War,
    D. Revolutionary War

17. A. explorer—
    B. explorer-
    C. explorer
    D. explorer,

18. A. , it has a poetic ring to it,
    B. —it has a poetic ring to it—
    C. , "it has a poetic ring to it,"
    D. : it has a poetic ring to it:

19. A. "The British Prison Ship".
    B. The British Prison Ship.
    C. "The British Prison Ship."
    D. , The British Prison Ship.

20. A. peoples
    B. people's
    C. peoples'
    D. peoples's

21. A. South Carolina, and Columbia, Missouri
    B. South Carolina; and Columbia, Missouri
    C. South Carolina and Columbia, Missouri
    D. South Carolina: and Columbia, Missouri

How Columbia inspired artists in the ___(22)___ The name appeared on coins, in patriotic paintings, and on the prows of ships. Most artists depicted Columbia as a ___(23)___ woman. Dressed in flowing robes, she wore a ___(24)___ and held an ___(25)___.

22. A. 1800s.
    B. 1800's.
    C. 1800s!
    D. 1800's!

23. A. tall stately
    B. tall, stately
    C. tall, stately,
    D. tall—stately—

24. A. star spangled cape
    B. star-spangled cape,
    C. star spangled cape,
    D. star-spangled cape

25. A. American Flag
    B. american flag
    C. American flag
    D. american Flag

Proofreading Practice: The Parts of Speech

Using Parts of Speech Correctly Read the following draft of a report. Then, using proofreading marks, correct the errors in capitalization, punctuation, usage, and spelling.

The name of the Game

Soccer is a game that has became more and more popular recently in the United States. Although it has been played for over two thousand years in other parts of the world. Versions of this sport, which is general known as football outside the United States, has been played in China, the Roman Empire, Britain, and Scotland.

The ancient Chinese played a game called *tsu chu,* which means "kick a ball of leather with the foot." This game was often played as entertainment for the emperor: and it could become vicious. The leader of the losing team was sometimes whipped.

The Romans played a game called *harpastium,* in which he kicked, punched, carried, or pushed the inflated bladder of an animal toward a goal. Many people thinks that the Romans brought kicking games to Britain, it wasn't until long after the Roman occupation ended, though, that these games were mentioned again in historical records.

Then, in the 800's, the British were fighting against Danish invaders and killed they're leader. The victorious British soldiers cut off the Danes head and kicked it through the village streets. That there day of victory became a annual National holiday with whole towns playing football. But not with human heads!

The game remained very violent, though, and punching, buting, and kicking were allowed. Playing football was good practice for the British soldiers, who often returned from war and went straight to the playing feild. Over the centuries the violence decrease, but no standard rules weren't developed until the 1800's.

At that time, several versions of football developed. One officially called Association Football or soccer. Another, in which a player could carry the ball in their hands, was called Rugby football. That's the forerunner of the American and Canadian Games as they are played today.

Proofreading Practice: The Sentence

Writing Correct Sentences Read the following draft of an advice column for a student newspaper. Correct all errors in capitalization, punctuation, usage, and spelling, paying particular attention to sentence structure. Use proofreading marks to indicate your changes.

Have you ever wondered why some people seem to have all the luck? And not others? They're are those who always seems to be in the right place at the right time. The rest of us arrive just after the nick of time or wander around, lost, for hours we are looking the other way when the big touchdown happens and miss the winning lottery number by one digit. We get to the bus stop just as the bus pulls away and step rite onto the only piece of half-chewed bubble gum stuck to the sidewalk anywhere nearby.

Well it doesn't have to be that way; you can make your own luck here's how. First, don't think "luck," think "look." You have to pay attention to whats going on around you. The person who gets the parking space is the one whose watching everything and anticipating what will happened next.

Second, Plan a head. If you always just miss your bus, leave home a few minute's early. If your the one who get splashed by passing cars when it's raining. Don't walk close to the curb; or wear a long raincoat. If you can't never manage to be in the right place at the right time, at least you can try not to be in the wrong place.

Finally, make the better of whatever happens to you. Luck is less happenstance than "happy stance." Someone once say, "If life hands you a lemon, make lemonade." Then if only the lemonade fill your glass halfway. Think of it as half full, not half empty, and consider yourself lucky.

Proofreading Practice: Phrases and Clauses

Using Phrases and Clauses Correctly Read the following draft of a business letter, paying particular attention to the phrases and clauses. Then use proofreading marks to correct all errors in capitalization, punctuation, usage, and spelling.

Abel N Cane

96 Juniper Court

Prairie, WI 55555

Oct 31, 19—

Mailing list Blockers

1771 Orchard Drive

Forest Ridge IA 50011

To Whom it may Concern:

 I found opening my mailbox the other day no less than seven advertisements and other pieces of junk mail. I as interested as anyone else in new products and services but this is getting ridiculous.

 For example, I recently read one of the promotional offers that came in the mail with my family. Cellophane-covered and unopened. I could see the message clearly through the envelope: "Abel N. Cane, you have just won one million dollars or current resident." Nobody isn't going to give away a million dollars through the mail. All I could think of was how many of these useless mailings had been sent out. To thoughtlessly use paper this way is not only stupid but environmentally irresponsible.

 I understand that the companies, which send out mail like these get names and addresses from mailing lists. I also have heard for a fee that your company has access to these mailing lists and can remove names from them.

 If this is true, please delete my name from all your lists and bill me without delay. Thank you very much.

Sincerely yours,

Abel N. Cane

Avoiding Incomplete Sentences As you read the following draft of part of a story, look for mistakes in capitalization, punctuation, usage, and spelling. Then correct the mistakes using proofreading marks.

Inner Sanctum

"Don't move." The voice said. I couldn't have budged even if I had wanted to I was paralyzed with terror.

Why hadn't I just stayed with the rest of the group. I had to be the wise guy, had to be the brave daredevil. Had to wander off on my own. I just couldn't resist. Following the dark, snaking corridor that I had noticed out of the corner of my eye when we had passed through the main chamber of the cave. Now what was going to happen?

"Who are you the voice hissed. Whispering close to my ear.

"Who—I mean, how—I mean, what do you mean?" I sputered.

"Do you see anyone else around here?" the voice snarled.

Collecting my courage and figuring I didnt have anything to loose because I was already a goner. I answered, "Actually I can't see no one at all, including myself. Its as dark as a cave in here."

"That's very funny. Leave it to me to find a comedian."

Well, now we know who *I* am, who are *you* I continued boldly"?

"That's for me to know. And you to find out." the voice gloated.

"Well, your obviously a great wit and a incredibly original thinker yourself," I shot back that response has a real ring to it. Maybe you could copyright it and get royalties. Whenever anyone else used it."

"I've had just about enough of your smart remarks."

Before the sound of those words had even died away. I felt a rush of cold air and a heavy blow along the side of my head and the left side of my body.

I woke up with a jolt on the floor beside my bed.

Proofreading Practice: Using Verbs

Using Verbs Effectively Read the following news report drafts that present two different views of the same event. Pay particular attention to the use of verbs. Use proofreading marks to correct all errors in capitalization, punctuation, usage, and spelling.

A. Using Verb Forms Correctly

Animal-rights extremists stage another angry demonstartion early this morning in front of MediCorps Laboratories in Galena. The protesters are demanding the immediate release of the animals used in MediCorps important medical research. When approached, one protester insist, "We haven't breaked any laws and we stay here as long as MediCorps continues to torture innocent animals."

According to Dr. Alyce Fay, a Researcher at MediCorps, "The use of animals for medical research saves human lifes. MediCorps are desparately trying to find cures for Cancer, birth defects and AIDS. I keep thinking That if any of those protesters were dying of cancer, they wouldn't be out there trying to free rats. Would a teenager really be willing to lie down his or her life just to save an animal's life?"

Despite threats by the demonstrators, MediCorps has gave its word to keep this lab open so that it's live-saving research can go on.

B. Correcting Verb Errors

Animal activists are picketing the high profitable MediCorps Laboratories. Their demonstrations have bringed attention to the lab's practice of using live dogs and monkeys in its controvercial research. Dr. Helen Watt a professor of bioethics who has spoke often in support of similar protests said, "The demonstrators have risen some important questions we want an impartial panel to decide whether the animals have been treated humanely or, better yet, whether experimentation with animals are even necessary for the labs research. Right now those decisions have been leaved to MediCorps, and unfortunately the company has showed that it can't be trusted."

Dr Alyce Fay, a researcher at MediCorps, respond, "We have the right to carry out our research any way we sees fit. The protesters are nothing but terrorist."

An activist replied, "MediCorps chosen its direction and we have chosen ours. We'll set out here until they free the captive animals inside."

Proofreading Practice: Subject-Verb Agreement

Making Subjects and Verbs Agree Read the following draft of a portion of a book review. Use proofreading marks to correct all errors in capitalization, punctuation, usage, and spelling.

Many of the books written about animal life is overly sentimental. However, a new book, *the Human Nature of Birds* by Theodore Xenophon Barber, PhD. Gives scientific evidence that there are almost no way to overestimate the capabilities of these remarkable creatures. The authors main point is that a bird, like human beings, have the ability to think, to have opinions, and to make choices. Making and using tools, expressing emotion and even creating music is not activities unique to people. A family of birds has interactions as complex as those of any human family. In fact, a bird can be a better freind to a person than another human being might be.

Here is one story that illustrates the author's point good. The story involves two parakeets, Blue Bird, and Blondie. Blue Bird was an unusually lively intelligent bird who seemed to enjoy life tremendously. Flying in complicated loops and zigzags were a favorite activity he also was a creative Singer and could use many English phrases correct. "Can I have some?" he would say when he wanted to try the food someone were eating. Blue bird was three years old when the female parakeet, Blondie, was introduced into the household the wild squawking and acrobatic flying that Blue Bird did when he saw her was obviously a sign of love at first sight. Blue Bird sang to Blondie and talked to her in both English and bird language. "Pretty little Blondie give me a kiss, he would say, bumping his beak against hers."

When Blue Bird died at age ten, Blondie became very depressed and completely ignored another male parakeet that had been brought in to keep her company. The seven years' Blue Bird and Blondie shared was full of caring and committment that few human couples achieves. The day Blondie died, the male bird that she had ignored and that had never talked to her before walked around and around the table where she was laying, saying sadly, "Poor Blondie. Sweet little Blondie.

Do this behavior seem incredible to you? If so, read the book soon and experience the human nature of birds for yourself.

Proofreading Practice: Using Pronouns

Using Pronouns Correctly Read the following drafts of two advertisements. Then use proofreading marks to correct all errors in capitalization, punctuation, usage, and spelling.

A. Choosing the Correct Pronoun

Are you a person to who others look for advice, or do they just look right past you? Many people find theirselves caught on a treadmill, unhappy with their work, worried about what everyone else are doing, and trying to do better than him or her.

If this describes you, your in luck. Just between you and I, there will never be a opportunity like this one again. In four short months you can become the confident director of your own fate, a person whom other people will envy and try to imitate. In a world where no one knows their own mind, you will stand out as somebody whom is special.

So don't delay. Send for the genuine original Self-Improvement Ego Builder today. It says in all the psychology books that you can be your worst enemy—or best friend. Which will you be? The choice is yours.

B. Correcting Pronoun Errors

What you are about to read is the words of a satisfied user of Radi-All tires, Mr. Jason Fleece. Him endorsing our product was entirely his own idea. This is what he sayed:

"Last April my freind and myself was driving. to an Intramural Soccer Competition in Argo, about sixty-five miles from our school. We were enjoing it, even though a tremendous thunder storm had blew up. All of a sudden the car hit a slippery patch and started to skid. We were terrified because this wasn't no television docudrama; this was really happening to him and I. The car spinned around three or four times before my friend gained control and could put on the breaks. Then, just like the commercials for Radi-All Tires promised, the car stopped on a dime. I'm convinced that neither him nor I would be alive today if we had been in a car with any other tires on it."

How much does the life of you and your family mean to you? Think about it when you buy new tires for your car.

Proofreading Practice: Using Modifiers

Using Modifiers Correctly Read the following minutes of a student council meeting. Then use proofreading marks to correct all errors in capitalization, punctuation, usage, and spelling.

The meeting was called to order by the student council president, Ellyn Wright at 12;15 PM Friday Febuary 13. Each of the sixteen regular members were present.

Mike Lewis then read the minutes of last weeks meeting and asked for any additions to be added. There weren't none, so the president called for commitee reports.

The presidents' day committee chairperson, Rob Nielsen, reported that the Juniors had collected more donations than any class. Preparations next Monday for the all-school assembly were progressing good, he said, but volunteers were still needed to type programs and act as usher. Rob asked anyone who might be interested to contact him before the close of school that there day. He thanked the junior class for it's support, saying, "These kind of responses is what school spirit is all about.

The Ecology Committee report was given by the committee Chairperson Maya Lopes. She said that the proposal of a Ecology-Begins-at-Home Workshop had been received enthusiastic by both students and teachers. Anyone who wants to participate in the preliminarily planning for this event. Should contact Maya.

The following items of new business were then proposed:

• the upcoming student council elections and the most efficientest way to handle nominations

• a new food service concession for the Cafeteria since the meals served there now taste so badly

• the need to keep the school open on week ends so students can have acess to the science laboratorys

Discussion of them issues was postponed until next week the meeting was ajourned by Ellyn Wright at 12:56.

Proofreading Practice: Capitalization

Capitalizing Correctly Read the following draft of the script for a travelogue. Then use proofreading marks to correct all errors in capitalization, punctuation, usage, and spelling.

Karibuni. That means "Welcome to you all" in kiswahili, the National language of Kenya. This east African country is a little smaller than the State of Texas but has almost twice it's population. Kenya is bordered by the Indian ocean on the east; Somalia, Ethiopia, and Sudan on the North; Uganda and lake Victoria on the west; and Tanzania on the south. The equator runs from east to west right through the middle of the country, and a huge gorge, the Great Rift valley, divides the country—and much of the rest of east Africa—from north to south.

Every type of climate can be found in Kenya, from the hot humid Coast to the chilly central highlands there is also every type of landform—from mountains such as mount Kenya the higher point in the country, to Lakes such as lake Victoria, the largest lake in the Continent of Africa. An abundant variety of wildlife can be found, from antelopes to zebras. and in huge numbers too. Anthropologists think that our earliest human ancestors lived in the area that is now Kenya. The current inhabitants belong to over forty Ethnic Groups about one fifth are members of the largest group, the Kikuyu. Other important groups are the Kalenjin, kamba, Luhya and Luo.

The pace of life in Kenya like that in much of Africa moves slow. Many of the people still live a nomadic life; moving often in search of food and water for their animals'. More and more people are moving to the citys, though, and the capitol, Nairobi, is as modern and sophisticated as any city in western Europe or America. You can even get a great Chicago-Style Pizza there! The Country has gone through difficult political and economic times, but the people are warm friendly, and optimistic after all, their National Motto is *hakuna matata*—"no problem."

Proofreading Practice: End Marks and Commas

Using Correct Punctuation Read the following draft of a journal entry. Help the writer prepare it for publication as part of an autobiographical novel by using proofreading marks to correct all errors in capitalization, punctuation, usage, and spelling.

Thurs Apr 27, 19—

Dear Diary

Yes. It finally happened he asked me to go to the dance this weekend. He called last night. I near died when mom said I had a phone call. "Hi he said in his soft sweet voice. Is this Tisa?" All I could do was gulp, and make stupid squeaking noises. Afraid that he would realize his mistake and hang up the phone. But believe it or not he didn't. He even seemed kind of nervous himself.

"Would you—I mean, Could you—I mean, do you want to come to the dance with me Saterday night" he said in a rush? Did I want to? Do birds fly? In fact I hadn't been thinking about almost nothing else for two weeks.

I didn't want to let him know that, though. So I swallowed silently and said as casual as I could "Saturday? Let me see. Sure, I think that would be okay". Its just a good thing we didn't have vision phones or else he would've seen how I was blushing, and probably even could've seen my heart pounding.

He sounded so happy, though and just kind of whooped, "It will? You mean you'll come? Wow. That's great."

Now. How will I ever be able to wait two hole days and nights till the dance. Well I guess I'll just have to some how. Theres really about 10000 things to do before then, though. first get my hair cut since it's so uneven, stringy and sloppy; second, find something to wear; and third and this is the hardest thing work on my conversation skills. I want to be able to talk about any topic but not just chatter on and on if you know what I mean it seems almost impossible doesn't it.

Anyway I guess I'd better get started. I'll try not to worry too much because after all, it's just a date. Just a date? I suppose it is, but its one, which means more than anything else to me, now. Wish me luck.

Proofreading Practice: Semicolons, Colons, and Other Punctuation

Punctuating Correctly Read the following draft of a friendly letter. Use proofreading marks to correct errors in capitalization, punctuation, usage, and spelling.

Dear Jeremy;

Have I got news for you! Remember the times when we got lost in the woods last summer? You told me then that I had a bad sense of direction. Well those days are over. My family and me went orienteering yesterday, and I learned how to read maps. My sense of direction is much better, now.

Orienteering—it reminds me of cross-country running because a person must travel long distances outdoors—is a timed sport. Have you ever heard of it. The goal of the sport is to move through a marked course in as littlest time as possible. An orienteer carry a topographic map as a guide it shows the different surfaces of the course: such as rivers, inclines, and flat grasslands. Sometimes orienteers use com passes to help them navigate.

When my family got to the starting grounds, we had to unload all of our equipment maps, hiking boots, backpacks, bug repellent, sack lunches. We divide into small groups and waited for the race to begin. It was scheduled to start promptly at 230 P.M. Mom, Nick and Sylvia called theirselves the Mighty Trailers dad, Ray, and me were the Magnificent Mappers. The race actually began a little late. We finally hit the trail at 245 P.M.

Trying to figure out how to read the map was hard; in fact my group got lost several times during the race. The two most challengng things we did were: wading across a fast stream and climbing a rocky hill. Fortunatly our map reading skills did improve. It took more than three hours to complete the course. We finished the race in one hundred eighty seven minutes!

Your cousin,

Maya

Proofreading Practice: Apostrophes and Quotation Marks

Using Apostrophes and Quotation Marks The following draft of a report includes errors in capitalization, punctuation, usage, and spelling. As you read the draft, identify the errors and use proofreading marks to correct each error.

The Seven Wonders' of the ancient World

The Seven Wonders of the Ancient World were a group of objects. Built by people between 3000 BC. and A.D. 476. they lay in an area along the Mediterranean Sea. Each of these wonder's were either extremely large or distinctive in some way.

The three pyramids of Egypt at Giza are the older of the ancient wonders. the pyramids were built between 2600 and 2500 B.C. and served as the Egyptian kings's tombs. "These Pyramids are a "must see" on any trip to Egypt, youll be sorry if you miss them." say several travel books'.

The Hanging Gardens of Babylon were located near what is now Baghdad, Iraq. They were probably built for one of King Nebuchadnezzars wife's around 600 B.C. A Babylonian priest, Berossus, said that "these gardens were about 75 feet above the ground and were watered by slaves' who lifted water from the Euphrates river."

The Temple of Artemis at Ephesus was the largest and most complex anceint temple. It was made entirely of marble and was supported by 106 columns who's height was 40 feet. The original temple was burned down in 356 B.C. was rebuilt and was destoryed again by Goths' in A.D 262.

They're are four other ancient wonders. They are Zeus's statue at Olympia which stood 40 feet high; the Mausoleum at Halicarnassus in Southwestern Turkey, a huge white marble tomb; the Colossus of Rhodes, a enormous bronze statue honoring the Greek Sun god Helios located near the greek Island of Rhodes in the Aegean Sea; and the 400-foot-tall Lighthouse of Alexandria on the island of Pharos near Alexandria Egypt. Unfortunately, these four structures have been destroyed over the years.